*W*eekly
*M*editations

One Week at a Time
One Day at a Time

DEBRA CAMPANY

ISBN 978-1-64114-570-1 (paperback)
ISBN 978-1-64114-849-8 (hardcover)
ISBN 978-1-64114-571-8 (digital)

Christian Faith Publishing, Inc.
832 Park Avenue
Meadville, PA 16335
www.christianfaithpublishing.com

Printed in the United States of America

CONTENTS

ACKNOWLEDGMENTS

I want to first and foremost thank God for molding me and using me as His vessel to bless individuals and to empower them to enter into their God-given destiny and purpose.

A special thank you to my covenant partners who have sown into me, believing in the vision and purpose that God has entrusted into my care. I could not have done it without your faithful support and encouragement.

To my amazing husband Ed, who has been putting up with me preaching to him for years, I love you more than I could ever show you. God gave us to each other, and as we continue to walk forward into all He has for both of us, I am grateful and thankful to always know that I can just be who I am and you are going to love me anyways. Thank you for always encouraging me and believing in me and the call that God has placed upon me. I love you.

To James and Jacki Blu, you both bring a song to my heart, and God has truly blessed me with children who love God and who love their Momma. Thank you for putting up with me because next to Dad, you both heard my preaching the most. I love you both and I look forward to watching as you pursue all God has for you in the future.

READY TO COMMIT?

This is a fifty-two-week collection of food for your spirit. During this time, I believe that God will speak to you and stir within you the deep desire to achieve all that He has called you to be for His kingdom. You will start to realize that there is a real purpose that God created you for and that with His help, you can obtain all the blessings that He has for you.

I strongly urge you to only read one meditation a week, so you will have time to meditate on how it applies to your life. God says to let Him transform you into a new person by transforming the way that you think.

Too often, we are so eager to read the next chapter in a book, we overlook what God is saying to us. I encourage you to seriously ponder what you read each week and allow the word of God to change you. Do not just read this book, but interact with it. Underline in it, highlight in it, and write your thoughts. Make it your book and personalize it.

The challenge is to stick to this for the next fifty-two weeks. Jump around and choose a topic from the contents that may speak to your current situation, but whatever you do, pick a weekly meditation that speaks to you and your life. Write your thoughts down and pray over what you read. Meditate on what you read and what God says to you.

The contract below is between you and God. By signing your name, you are making a commitment not only to God, but to yourself.

God bless you as you start this journey into new revelation.

MY COVENANT

Lord, I commit myself to spending time with you every day, no matter what the cost. I am depending on your strength to help me to be consistent. With your help, I commit the next fifty-two weeks of my life meditating on your word and listening to your voice speak to me through these weekly meditations.

_____

Your name

A MESSAGE FROM
REVEREND DEBRA

My goal is to provide you with a weekly meditation that you can meditate on. My prayer is that as you meditate on a daily basis, God will open your spiritual eyes and speak into your life, and not only will you receive revelation concerning your life, but that it will transform your normal day into a catalyst for change. Be blessed and remember to pursue your destiny with all your passion.

Find Reverend Debra online: www.dcministriesinc.com

To begin your journey, turn the page.

DARE TO LIVE YOUR DREAM

Dare to live your dream in this season. Do not put your God-given dream on the shelf because you do not think it has a chance of being fulfilled. Do not give up due to the state of the economy, the state of your situation, or areas in your life in which you are falling short. Do not settle for what you think is God's best for you; instead press through toward God's best and the dream that He has given you.

Philippians 2:12–16 (AMP) reads:

> *Therefore, my beloved, as you have always obeyed, not as in my presence only, but now much more in my absence, work out your own salvation with fear and trembling: for it is God who works in you both to will and to do for His good pleasure. Do all things without complaining and disputing, that you may become blameless and harmless, children of God without fault in the midst of a crooked and perverse generation, among whom you shine as lights in the world, holding fast the word of life, so that I may rejoice in the day of Christ that I have not run in vain or labored in vain.*

I, myself, have been going through a very interesting situation, and someone else is at the helm, which makes it even more interesting because I cannot make the decisions. Yet the decisions that are being made do affect me personally. I am not in control of the decisions, so I actually see the situation differently than the person who is in control. I ran through different scenarios of what could happen, just like the person who has to make the decision would. Even though we are in different roles, we both have to trust God. I have to work out my own salvation (life), just like the other person has to work out his or hers.

Here is the bottom line: are we looking at what possibly could happen if we make a decision? Are we listening to what God is telling us to do and trusting Him with what could happen? Or are we so caught up in trying to figure out the walking-through part (even that of the other person) that we are missing what is being whispered in our ears? Are we focusing on who would be affected by the decision rather than focusing on God and trusting Him? Through our obedience, He has already worked all things out for our good. As long as we continue to listen and obey, He will maneuver us through this obstacle course called our life.

We have to dare to live the dream that God has placed within us, trusting Him that as we walk in obedience to His word and work out our own salvation that He will make the crooked ways straight. We have got to stop looking at, listening to, and acting upon what people say, and look at, listen to, and act upon what God says.

Are you settling for your version of your dream being fulfilled, or are you pressing on for what you know God asks of you concerning your dream, your destiny?

I dare you to live your dream.

Meditation Thought

I challenge you that:

No matter who may be at the helm of certain situations in your life, you still continue to press in to possess your God-given dreams and visions.

I challenge you to:

Examine how you are addressing the situations in your path. Are you in control of them (making your own decisions) or are you being led by God concerning them? Are you making decisions based on obedience to what you believe He is saying to you?

Life is challenging in itself right now, but that does not mean you have to set down your God-given dream and destiny. You need to pursue, press on, and push forth into God's destiny for your life. I challenge you not to settle, but rather set your course and run the race before you!

My Thoughts

_____

_____

_____

_____

_____

_____

_____

_____

_____

_____

_____

_____

_____

_____

_____

_____

_____

_____

PREPARE THE WAY

God began to show me that just as we prepare for events in our life, we have to prepare for God seasons. By doing this, we prepare the way for Him to be able to operate fully in our lives.

I, myself, had to go to storage and take out certain items in order to have them ready and available to decide what to keep and what to get rid of. When we prepare for God's season, it is the same principle. We sometimes have to go into our storage unit (our mind, our will, and our emotions) and take some things out and look at them. We need to decide what we can use now, use another time, and what we need to get rid of in order for Him to be able to do what He desires to do in our lives.

Sometimes, the things we think are the most complicated to accomplish are really quite simple. We complicate them by overthinking them, putting them off, or delaying them because of excuses. If we begin to recognize that our whole life and the choices we make on a daily basis are actually part of our preparation process, then maybe when God is specific with us about what we need to do to prepare, we would be quicker to obey His voice.

In 1 Corinthians 2:9–10 (NKJV) is one of many examples of preparation in the word. It reads:

> *Eye has not seen, nor ear heard, Nor have entered into the heart of man The things which God has prepared for those who love Him.*

God has already prepared everything for those who love Him. Verse 10 reads:

But God has revealed them to us through His Spirit.

Could this possibly mean that as God reveals these things (His plan, His dream, His will) to us, that we, out of our love for Him, obey His voice? Then all the things God has prepared for us will manifest in our lives because we are walking according to His lead. We have to know that it is all a process.

How do we prepare the way? By doing what we do to prepare for anything in our life. We have to have a plan! When you fail to plan, you plan to fail. Our parents prepared for our birth. They prepared for us to go to kindergarten. Some prepared for us to go to college and then marry. We prepared ourselves for school and for activities in which we were involved. We prepared to take tests. We prepare for the holidays. We prepare to go to work. We prepare for family get-togethers or to travel. Some people even prepare to overcome fears in order to travel. The list can go on and on and on.

Do you recognize what is happening here? Our life is one big preparation! My prayer is that my life is one big preparation to fulfill God's will and destiny for my life—what about yours? Is God dealing with you concerning your preparation process? Has He been specific with you about people, places, and things in your life that you may need to walk away from or walk into? Is fear keeping you from obeying his voice in preparing the way? Is there something in your own thought pattern that is beating you up and keeping you from thinking you are worthy to love in God's preparation process?

Do not fret! He already knows what you are facing in your preparation process. Remember, nothing in your life surprises, shocks, or deters God from His love for you or His desire for you to manifest that which you have prepared your whole life for! He has already factored all of this into His master plan—His master timetable for you. Do not cry over spilled milk—wipe it up! Keep on going, and remember, everything you have been through, are going through, and will go through is all part of your preparation process. So run the race set before you. Do not quit and do not disqualify yourself. God has not!

Meditation Thought

Look at your life as preparing the way for you to fulfill God's will in your life. If you look at your life as a mess, God is using that mess to become your message.

Change the way you see your life and look at it through the eyes of God. If you do not know how He sees your life, read 3 John 2. If you are around negative people, take a time out and get around people who will build you up.

You have but this one life here on earth, so I challenge you to live it to God's fullest!

My Thoughts

_____
_____
_____
_____
_____
_____
_____
_____
_____
_____
_____
_____
_____
_____
_____
_____
_____
_____

MAINTAINING BALANCE
IN UNBALANCED TIMES

How do you maintain balance in unbalanced times? By remembering to keep God first. When we are faced with uncertainty, we have a tendency to enter into a crisis or survival mode, which causes us to forget everything except what we are facing. This is not good for us. When we enter into this mode, we begin to become unbalanced. We drop this and we drop that; we toil and twist and turn, trying to figure out if we should go this way or that way. One of the first things to go is the amount of time we spend with God. Maybe you spent an hour daily with Him, journaling, praying, meditating, and listening to what He had to say to you. Now, because of the circumstances that surround you, you dropped your time with Him to a half hour and you don't get to sit quietly any longer. You don't get to listen to your favorite teaching tapes because even when you are in your car, your mind is racing, trying to determine what to do with the circumstances you are facing. You know that you are out of balance, yet you are not quite sure you want to let go of your mode because it is actually comforting to you. You are in an unbalanced state, and I hear God saying, "Whoa!" I just got a vision of him pulling on your reigns and telling you to "stop—I got it!"

"Reverend Debra, how do I maintain balance when everything is going every which way around me?"

Let's look at the word. Mark 4:35–41 (AMP) reads:

On that same day when evening had come, He said to them, let us go over to the other side of the lake. And leaving the throng, they took Him with them, just as He was, in the boat in which He was sitting. And other boats were with Him. And a furious storm of wind, of hurricane proportions arose, and the waves kept beating into the boat, so that it was already becoming filled. But He himself was in the stern of the boat, asleep on the leather cushion; and they awoke Him and said to Him, Master, do You not care that we are perishing? And He arose and rebuked the wind and said to the sea, Hush now! Be still; muzzled! And the wind ceased; sank to rest as if exhausted by its beating and there was immediately a great calm, a perfect peacefulness. He said to them, why are you so timid and fearful? How is it that you have no faith, no firmly relying trust? And they were filled with great awe and feared exceedingly and said one to another, who then is this, that even wind and sea obey Him?

The storm was beating not only their ship, but all of the other little ships that were with them. They were being tossed by the waves. Notice Jesus was asleep in the ship with them, but He was at rest on a pillow. They were in the crisis (fear), and they woke Jesus up and asked Him, "Master, don't you care that we are going through this and we are not going to make it?"

Jesus got up and He didn't rebuke the waves, He rebuked the cause of the waves—the wind. He spoke to the sea, "Peace, be still."

When you are unbalanced, you are fearful, and you are trying to deal with the result instead of the cause of the tossing about. Jesus clearly shows us in this passage that we are to deal with the cause and tell the symptoms to line up.

Meditation Thought

I want to encourage you to use this passage as an example of how to maintain balance in unbalanced times. Is Jesus in your ship with you?

Or did you drop Him off at the first toss about? Only you know the answer to this question, and I want to encourage you to examine yourself in order to determine if Jesus is in your ship. If He is, then it is good.

If you discover you may have pushed Him overboard, not to worry, because Jesus is a water-walker! Just reach over and help Him back into your ship and watch the balance begin to manifest once again!

My Thoughts

I'M COMING OUT!

In order for us to come out, we have to know what the secret is to accomplishing this. Are you ready to find out what that secret is?

The secret to coming out is change! That's right, change! You have to have courage to change. The definition of *change* (dictionary.com) is: *to transform or convert, to become different, to become altered or modified.* The only way to change your life is if you make a decision to do so. No one else can do it for you, not even God himself. You have to have the courage to be redeveloped and to be transformed. You were developed one way due to your upbringing, your circumstances, your situations in life, and it is up to you to go back into the darkroom and come out redeveloped. Your darkroom is your test or trial. To *redevelop (dictionary.com) means: to develop something again, to improve a rundown area—to make better use of wasteland— encourage inward investment.*

Romans 12:2 (KJV) reads:

> *Do not conform any longer to the pattern of this world, but be transformed by the renewing of your mind.*

I believe what this scripture is saying is to no longer conform to your ideas, your patterns, your perceptions, but be transformed (changed) by renewing your mind. It is all about change.

In simpler words, when you are going through a dark place in your life, it is because you are in the redevelopment process. You are being changed into a more toned you. OK, let me go a little deeper.

Some of you have stuff inside of you that is rotten and you can feel it. You can smell it, and it makes you sick and rundown emotionally, physically, and spiritually. It is time to rip it out, to tear it down, to renovate it, and to replace it with the fresh newness of God that is in you. It is time for you to become a clearer, brighter picture of your former self. If you have Christ in you, you are a new creation. The old things pass away. How, you ask? By dealing with it!

Let us enter the darkroom and come out when God says it is time—not before or after—but in obedience to God. So ask yourself a very honest question: what is holding me back from becoming all that God has for me? Do not look at your spouse, your children, your circumstances, and so on. These are all excuses, and the only thing holding you back is you! You have dreams inside of you that you thought were dead. They are not dead. They have been lying dormant in the tomb, waiting for you to come out. We have to take notice of what our dreams were when we were children. Many of you have laid down your passions for one reason or another. Pick them back up, walk with them, and allow God to use them as an avenue to your prosperity. Be obedient to God. Just because you had to put your talents or gifts up on a shelf for a season does not mean they are permanently shelved. Listen for Him to declare to you that you are coming out and pick them up off the shelf and begin to walk with them.

Meditation Thought

Coming out is a process, and if you come out too soon, you will be underdeveloped. If you come out too late, you will be overdeveloped.

God wants us out when we are developed, and that comes from listening and doing what He tells us to do.

John 11:43 (NIV) says:

Jesus called in a loud voice, Lazarus, come out.

Jesus is calling to you right now, "Come out. I want to resurrect you. I want you to be loosed and walk in all I have promised you, but just like Lazarus you have to listen, hear, and obey the voice of God and walk out."

I believe that I hear footsteps—it is you, man or woman of God, coming out!

My Thoughts

_____

_____

_____

_____

_____

_____

_____

_____

_____

_____

_____

_____

_____

_____

_____

_____

_____

_____

_____

CHANGE

Many of us are going through changes in our lives. Some of us are just going with the flow, and others are having a difficult time adjusting to the changes.

The definition of *change* (dictionary.com) is: *transform, convert, to make the form, nature, content, future course, of (something) different from what it is or from what it would be if left alone.*

Romans 12:2 (NKJV) reads:

> *And do not be conformed to this world, but be transformed by the renewing of your mind, that you may prove what is that good and acceptable and perfect will of God.*

Change (transformation) is a part of our life. I know many of you are facing very difficult situations right now. Your home may be in foreclosure, you may not have any income, you may be facing a personal disappointment, or any other number of seemingly insurmountable issues in life. I want to encourage you to look below the surface of the circumstance and seek God as to what He is doing in your life. It appears to be headed in one direction, but when you know that you are being obedient to what God is directing you to do, it is nothing like what it appears to be on the surface. I have had to learn to look beneath the surface of my circumstances and see them through God's eyes. Your obedience during these times is critical because your emotions may try to rule you. Do what you have to do to get your emotions under subjection to your spirit (cry, scream, write, pray, or whatever your release is), and then grab the bull by the horns and look into its eyes and say, "I can do all things through Christ who strengthens me!" Pull yourself up and keep walking through the changes.

A great example of change is when women go through menopause. Their bodies change and they don't have control over what their bodies are doing. They have to do what is healthy for them holistically or medically. They seek guidance and direction. What is different between women seeking guidance and direction when their bodies go through change and when our lives go through change? Nothing! We have to seek guidance from God, from someone we trust, or even an expert in the given field. Please don't misunderstand me and share with someone who cannot help you. Only share with someone who can help you discover the answer you are seeking from God.

Meditation Thought

We need each other more than ever in this season, and I want to encourage you that you are not alone in what you are facing.

Many individuals are experiencing change in their lives; some are handling it better than others. I know that you can come through every trial, every setback, and say that you can do all things through Christ who strengthens you. Do not get stuck in your transformation (change), and do not become paralyzed by it. Do what needs to be done, and when you have done everything you believe God has directed you to do, stand and see the salvation (the work) of the Lord!

I Am is with you!

My Thoughts

_____

_____

_____

_____

_____

_____

_____

_____

_____

_____

_____

_____

_____

_____

_____

_____

_____

_____

_____

_____

LIFESTYLE

Lifestyle. That word is very powerful and has a different definition for each and every one of us. My lifestyle requires certain things from me and from those around me, yet it is my perception of how I choose to live my life. I asked God why He would give me such a broad topic to discuss, and His response was "I want my people to examine their lives and to prune off the unnecessary branches that they have been carrying because of the lifestyle they have chosen."

People, God loves you, yet there are times when we all have too much going on in our lives and it pushes aside the things that truly matter. If you are a single parent, there are a lot of responsibilities that you carry; a married woman also carries a lot of responsibilities, yet they are not the same. Each of us has to determine what is important in our lives and let go of the unnecessary branches that take away from the ability to maintain a healthy mental altitude. Your lifestyle is a mental attitude, and your *attitude* determines your *altitude*. I could have nothing in my bank account and still know how to make the adjustments needed to remain joyful. I would not lose the altitude of my mental attitude because I know it is only temporary. I *know* God always allows pruning to take place in order for new growth to occur. Once we know this, the adjustment period becomes smoother. (Notice I said smoother, not necessarily easier—because flesh dies.)

There are those of you who right now are struggling spiritually, financially, emotionally, or physically. Nevertheless, you have not allowed the circumstances to deter you from maintaining the altitude of your mental attitude. You may have been shaken and had to digest what was taking place, yet you pulled yourself up by the bootstraps and kept on going. You are making the adjustments that you believe God is asking you to make, and you *know* that it is all going to work out for your good.

Then there are those of you who are struggling with the same things, yet you have no idea that there is light at the end of the tunnel. I want to minister especially to you. It is going to be OK. Tap into your creative side. It is there, but because of the things that have built up in your life, you may not have used that side of you for a while. I have recently gone through a pruning process, but through the process, I have been able to tap into my creative side and discover ideas that I have not had to use for years. Because of this, I am able to prune what needs to be cut off and use the gifts within me that have lain dormant for years. (Notice I said dormant, not dead.)

Meditation Thought

We have to be willing to do whatever it takes to adjust our lifestyle to God's lifestyle for us. Remember, for everything there is a season.

We have to be able to adjust into the season we are experiencing in our lives. For example, we have winter clothes and summer clothes. We have to be obedient and willing to listen to and do what God says to do with our lifestyle and to change our clothes for the season we are in.

We can make a serious mistake in our pruning process if we look at the loss as something bad instead of looking at it as God pruning it from our life because He knows we will not need it in our next season.

God moves us from glory to glory, and the only way we can continue to gain altitude is by going through the pruning process and leaving behind the branches that we no longer need to survive and soar higher than we ever have. Walk forth, people of God! Walk out with an *attitude of altitude* Don't allow the cares of this world to deter you from entering your next level of glory, and do not fear what God tells you to prune away!

My Thoughts

IMPRISONED BY ACTIONS:
YOURS OR SOMEONE ELSE'S

In Acts 16:16–39, Paul and Silas were thrown into prison (into their circumstance, their situation, their issue). Paul was greatly annoyed by the girl following them for days and crying out, saying, "These men are the servants of the most high God, who proclaims to us the way of salvation."

Her deliverance came when Paul was at his highest point of frustration. Yet Silas's imprisonment, Silas's bondage also came at Paul's highest point of frustration, one was set free and one was put into bondage.

Once the girl's masters found out she was of no use to their fortunetelling business, they seized Paul *and* Silas and dragged them into the marketplace to the authorities. They brought them before the magistrates and said, "These men, being Jews, exceedingly trouble our city; and teach customs which are not lawful for us, being Romans, to receive or observe" (v. 20).

Then the multitude rose up against Paul and Silas. The magistrates stripped them and commanded them to be beaten with rods and whipped them and threw them into prison. The magistrates commanded the jailer to keep them securely imprisoned. The jailer then proceeded to put them in the inner prison and fastened their feet in stocks.

Their joint imprisonment came about because of Paul's actions. Can you imagine Silas just standing there going through this process with Paul and knowing that he had to trust God to move on his behalf? Silas was imprisoned because of someone else's actions—Paul's. Yet God had this situation already worked out for Paul's and Silas's (and others') good.

Do you understand that your actions not only affect you but they affect those around you? Sometimes, we think that it is just about us. It is not. This is a powerful example of that. It is bad enough that sometimes our own choices imprison us, but I have come to realize that my words, focus, and actions *do* affect those people I cross paths with in my daily life.

Silas was not given the choice to walk away, and the crowd did not say, "Silas—you didn't do these things, it is all Paul." No, they grouped the two of them together. They put them both in prison because the girl's masters made it appear one way when it was really another. They were angry about losing their profits, and they used what Paul had done against both Paul and Silas. Has this ever happened to you? Have you been imprisoned by someone else's choices or words? Do you feel that your destiny has been delayed because of another individual? It's OK! Don't focus on how to get out of the imprisonment. Rather, do what Paul and Silas did in prison. They sought God, and, as they did, those around them listened and watched them. Here they were in what appeared to be a dungeon, and God was still their focus.

People are watching you—even the ones who you may feel are holding you back. Do you realize that you can move forward even if it appears every situation in your life is working against you and you keep hitting walls? Paul and Silas were surrounded by walls and locked in chains, yet because they focused on God, the world around them shook and the chains came off (not just Paul's and Silas's but those around them). The doors opened and their enemy (the jailer) fell at their feet and asked them, "How do I?"

I need to ask again—do you realize your choices, actions, focus, etc., affect those around you? For better or worse, those around you are affected by your focus, and your focus determines your choices. I challenge you this week to focus on God and *not* the situation that is in your life. As you focus on God, He will show you where you need to walk. Be bold, be strong, and be gentle on yourself in this process.

God already has worked it out for your good, but you have to decide to focus on Him and walk in obedience to what He is telling you to do and not to do!

Meditation Thought

I am focusing on God this week and I am allowing Him to order my footsteps.

I challenge you that as you focus on God and He begins to give you direction on how to break the chains off your feet that you will be obedient to His voice.

Proclaim this: "I will not fear what man can do to me! God has ordered my footsteps and all things are working together for my good!"

My Thoughts

_____
_____
_____
_____
_____
_____
_____
_____
_____
_____
_____
_____
_____
_____
_____
_____
_____
_____

SEE BEYOND THE THREAT

During one prayer meeting I attended, the leader spoke about Ahab and Jezebel. The leader shared many great thoughts, but one in particular spoke to me. He made the statement, "He (Ahab) failed to see beyond the threat" (1 Kings 19:3–4)! Jezebel was a master intimidator, and where there is a threat, there is intimidation. Where there is intimidation, there is an area inside of us that we have to reflect on because we aren't supposed to be intimidated by anyone—was God?

I want to ask you a question. Do you see beyond the threat? You may be threatened with any one of or a combination of the following issues: financial, physical, emotional, marriage difficulties, spiritual questioning, etc. Do you see beyond the threat? Or is all your attention focused on the threat? Could it possibly be that the threat you are facing is someone else's idea of how you should be approaching a circumstance or situation in your life? I want to challenge you to be honest with yourself. If you are focused on the threat, use this week to refocus on listening to God's voice concerning your situation and to gain an understanding of why you are feeling threatened.

When a threat comes into our path, we may feel some of these emotions: intimidation, fear, confusion, belittlement, anxiety, etc. If we do not see beyond the threat, we can enter into manipulation and deception due to our emotions. If you are manipulating a circumstance to work out for you, you are only deceiving yourself. It is not God, it is you doing it in your flesh, and you will reap what you sow (hence a cycle of trouble). If you take time to seek God concerning a circumstance, and as He directs you and you are obedient to that direction, it will all work out for your good (whether it appears that way or not). It will!

When you see the threat, it causes you to move in your own strength and reasoning. When you see beyond the threat, it causes you to move in God's strength and mind-set.

I want to use the credit card companies as an example of a threat. You have fallen behind due to the economic situation and they call you continually, but you choose to ignore their call. You are ignoring their phone calls because you do not want to deal with the situation, and you see them as a threat. You are not dealing with this situation quite possibly because of fear, due to ignorance of what you should tell them, or due to your insecurity or being ashamed that you are in this situation. Not dealing is not God! We are to be people of integrity, which means, pick up the phone. Give them a brief description of why you cannot make your payment, and if you do not know what you are going to do, be honest with them and don't make promises you cannot keep. Making promises you cannot keep puts more pressure on yourself. Do not ignore these phone calls because they will not go away. They are no longer a threat because you have taken away their power by confronting them according to God's leading. You can now answer the phone and deal with them on your terms. The freedom is yours!

When your mind-set is pointed in the right direction, you see beyond the threat and are able to face the threat with both barrels loaded with God power!

Meditation Thought

I challenge you to:

See beyond the threat.

Look at why you are choosing not to deal with the threat. If your life was threatened, you would do whatever you knew you needed to do to protect yourself. You would use every resource available to you and you would seek counsel if you did not know what to do. So why wouldn't you do this concerning all areas of your life?

Not run from confrontation, but rather, seek God on what His direction is concerning confronting these threats, these obstacles, and these distractions in your life.

My Thoughts

_____
_____
_____
_____
_____
_____
_____
_____
_____
_____
_____
_____
_____
_____
_____
_____
_____
_____
_____

STOP SEEING OBSTACLES;
SEE STEPPING STONES

It is time to stop seeing obstacles and see stepping stones. If we are focusing on the obstacles then we are focusing on the limits in our life. If we stop seeing the obstacles as obstacles and start seeing them as stepping stones, we have just made the first step in overcoming these limits. What do you see? Do you see the obstacle as a negative happening, or do you see it as an opportunity for you to grow?

God showed me that we have got to recognize the limits we have imposed upon ourselves and those that others have imposed upon us. Are you ready? Are you ready to face these obstacles and step on them as God intended us to? His word tells us the enemy is under our feet—a great stepping-stone.

Let's look at Jesus. When he was faced with the obstacle of Lazarus's death, he could have turned around and walked away. He chose not to walk away, however, and he continued to move forward and faced that obstacle. He told Lazarus to come out, and out Lazarus came. Jesus took what was an obstacle and created a stepping-stone. He didn't stop moving forward.

People, we have to have a conviction on the inside of us that no matter what comes across our path, we will look at it as an opportunity for us to grow and use it as a stepping-stone to our destiny. It is your choice and your decision. Some may have to take a time-out, but don't let the time-out become an excuse to get out of the race. You will only have to rerun it. So why not press, push, and pursue this time around? Use that obstacle as a stepping-stone. Allow your thoughts about it to be transformed, and you will see the obstacle as a step into your destiny!

It is time to stop seeing the obstacles and to take off the limits. God says we can do all things through Christ who strengthens us. Stop living only in your power and make a decision to trust and obey what God is saying to you. He is speaking! It is time to stop seeing the obstacles and trust God with every step you take or nothing will change.

Your life is in His hands and He will reveal His plan as you use what you used to see as obstacles as stepping-stones instead.

Meditation Thought

I challenge you to:

Change the way you see an obstacle and make the choice today that everything that was interfering with your success is no longer in your way because you now see obstacles as stepping-stones, and they are under your feet.

My Thoughts

_____
_____
_____
_____
_____
_____
_____
_____
_____
_____
_____
_____
_____
_____
_____
_____
_____
_____
_____
_____

ENJOY THE MOMENTS

You may be experiencing stress this week or even loneliness, I want to challenge you that whatever you may be enduring this week that you enjoy the moments. Enjoy all the moments God gives you: the little blessings, the sweetest hello, the small smile you receive or give. Enjoy the moment that you are experiencing even if you feel it is the worst one ever. Look for the smallest blessings in it.

Circumstances and situations may not always work out the way you think they should. But God already has it worked out for you. Could it be that He is protecting you from something detrimental to your well-being? Possibly, He sees a greater blessing coming to you and is asking you to give up that one thing you have been holding on to.

I challenge you this week to use it as an opportunity to practice enjoying the moment that you are in. Don't be in such a rush that you miss what God is doing for you and in you.

I know what He has been saying to me—the simpler, the better. I have done things that I haven't done in years. For example, I used to love to bake, but I set it aside and it became a last priority as I got too busy with other things. I made the decision that I was going to bake something even if I didn't make it from scratch. It is the little goals that we set and accomplish that help us to achieve the bigger goals. God's word says that when we are faithful with the little things, He is going to bless us. Take time to recognize the small things—the little moments in time—that you have been missing due to the stress, the loneliness, or the busyness of your life.

The decision is yours.

Meditation Thought

I challenge you to:

Enjoy the moment(s) that you will walk into this week.

I challenge you to:

Do one thing that you used to enjoy doing, but because of busyness, stress, or loneliness, you have set it aside.

Choose to enjoy the moments, however small, that come into your life!

My Thoughts

_____
_____
_____
_____
_____
_____
_____
_____
_____
_____
_____
_____
_____
_____
_____
_____
_____
_____
_____
_____
_____

YOUR VISION AND GOALS

There are those of you who have a vision for life. Because of the vision, you have established goals, and you know how to work the principle I am going to share. This may be a refresher course for some of you. There are those of you who are not sure what your vision is or how to establish goals. So this week, I will share a few principles concerning your vision and goals.

Your vision is your passion. It is that thing that never leaves you, the thing that you dream of accomplishing. It is right before you. It may be a dream of owning your own business, working in the ministry, traveling in missions, helping those less fortunate than yourself, teaching, or going back to school for that degree you always wanted. Whatever you have dreamed of and are passionate about is your vision.

You must write your vision down (Habakkuk 2:2–3) so that he may run who reads it. Your vision is that dream—what you desire to do with your life. Writing it down is the first step to manifesting it in the natural. Writing it down is the key that unlocks the spiritual aspect of it and brings it into the natural realm.

If you cannot write your vision down, then you are not earnest about it. If you can't take the time to write it down, you really don't want it. Writing down your vision and goals helps focus you in that direction. Writing them down and keeping them before you on a daily basis will help you to maintain that focus.

If you are truly committed to your goals, if you have a true passion about your vision and you want it more than anything, it means God's destiny is being fulfilled in your life.

51

I write affirmations in my journal daily, and I have my monthly goals as well as yearly goals. I keep them in my journal and look at them daily. I have seen God fulfill goal after goal, and I know it is because I have written them down. Through that, I have remained focused on what His destiny is for my life.

Write them down and run.

Meditation Thought

I challenge you to:

Do this one thing as you prepare for the coming week—write down your goals, your vision. Make it plain, read it, and then run with it.

My Thoughts

_____
_____
_____
_____
_____
_____
_____
_____
_____
_____
_____
_____
_____
_____
_____
_____
_____
_____
_____
_____
_____

FOCUSED ON FAITH

Many of us may be facing challenges in our lives. I want to encourage you to be focused on faith. It's quite easy to focus on the fears in our lives, but that is the opposite of faith. Faith is the substance of things hoped for and the evidence of things not yet seen. Faith is action. Fear is the opposite of faith, and when fear is in operation, faith is not. Fear paralyzes you if you allow it to. Faith will propel you forward.

I have found that there are many faces of fear. It can manifest in anger and tears, in that sick-to-your-stomach feeling, and in health issues. The list can go on and on. It does help if we are able to recognize these manifestations and nip them in the bud. Of course, in a perfect world, that would be simple, right? But we are not in a perfect world, nor are we perfect. We are in process. I personally had to go through the fear process in order to refocus and remain focused on faith.

We have to be gentle with ourselves and understand our own processing of the data that is a part of our lives. If we are willing to take a look at this data, we will then allow ourselves to not get caught up in the fear. When the fear appears, we will be able to process it and remain focused on faith.

"Reverend Debra, you keep saying 'focused on faith.' What do you mean exactly?"

I mean, having the ability to remain focused on the necessary action (faith) needed to continue movement in our lives, even when we are faced with the fear of failure, rejection, hurts, health issues, financial issues, family issues, and so on. That is "focused on faith."

You can know every scripture in the word pertaining to fear and faith, but unless you remain focused on faith, they are just words that you are quoting. Your faith (action) is dead because there are no works (movement), and faith without works is dead.

I encourage you to continue to press forward even in the midst of your circumstances. If you need to take a break, take one, but don't linger there any longer than what you believe God is telling you to.

Get up and keep focused on faith and move into your divine destiny and purpose!

Meditation Thought

I challenge you to:

Admit the fears you are facing. Go through your process and then focus on faith. The next time fear shows itself, you will be able to remain focused on faith and not become paralyzed by the fear.

I challenge you to:

Not fear the process, but rather process the fear, so you are able to be focused on faith.

I challenge you to:

Get up and move forward into your divine destiny!

My Thoughts

_____
_____
_____
_____
_____
_____
_____
_____
_____
_____
_____
_____
_____
_____
_____
_____
_____
_____
_____

YOUR WORD

What is commitment? The Bible tells us to let our yes be yes and our no be no. Your word is your commitment to do that which you have said you will do. A lot of us commit to things just because, and then we end up not following through on our commitments. This is an obstacle to having the ability to fulfill our destiny. You have to learn that it is OK to say no.

I would first have to challenge you to take a look at why you say yes to everything and are afraid to say no. I was one of those people (a people pleaser), and I would overcommit myself and end up so bogged down by the busyness in my life that I had no room for me and what God wanted me to do. I believe that many people do not even realize that they do this. They lack the understanding of the "why" behind the "do."

We have to learn to say no, and we have to realize it is not selfish to do so. Do not let anyone put guilt on you for saying no! Come away from a people-pleasing lifestyle and into a God-pleasing one. You will reap mightily when you live a life of obedience to Him. Please understand that I am talking about your personal life. When you are at work and your boss asks you to do a task, do not say no because you don't feel like doing it. We are dealing with you personally!

When you renew your mind to let your yes be yes and your no be no, you open yourself up to a new level of glory in God. He can now trust you with your word. Do you see how important your word is?

When I was going through my renewal process, there were instances where I had committed to something I couldn't really fulfill. When I realized what I had done, I had to go and apologize. I had to say that I couldn't fulfill my commitment. It was so much better than making up some lie about why I couldn't do it or why I didn't show up. This was a great lesson for me because it taught me that it is better to be a person of integrity and admit when I make an error than it is to just not show up or show up with the wrong attitude.

Make this your week of mastery by mastering your word.

Meditation Thought

I challenge you to:

Examine yourself and the "why" behind your "do."

I challenge you to:

Say no to that one thing that you really can't commit to and only would agree to in order to please someone else. Let your yes be yes and your no be no.

I challenge you to:

Live a "God-pleaser" life!

I challenge to:

Live by your word and be what He wants for you and your destiny!

Come on, challenge yourself!

My Thoughts

REST IN HIM

God is asking us to rest in Him. Those things you have begun will be accomplished but not in your timing, in His timing.

How do you rest in Him? By knowing that you have done everything that you can do pertaining to the situation and then just standing. When we stand, we are still, and He tells us, "Be still and know that I am God." Our problem is in being still long enough for Him to be God in our circumstances.

At some point in our walk with God, we come to the realization that we cannot do anymore. In that realization comes the freedom to rest in Him. This does not necessarily mean we lay down and take a nap (even though that is the best thing we can do sometimes), it means we have peace in the midst of the storm. Anything that we are going through is exactly that—going through. It is temporary. The part that disturbs us is not knowing exactly how it is going to work out or how it is going to end.

We can have reassurance from God that everything is going to be OK and all things are working together for our good. Yet until we can come to a place of resting in the knowing that He is in control and all we have to do is be obedient, we will be unsettled and restless.

For some strange reason, we have a problem with not knowing, yet He tells us to walk by faith and not by sight. When we walk by faith, we are not walking and stepping on the solid ground in the natural realm, but rather the solid ground in the spiritual realm.

The only way we are going to know what that solid, spiritual ground is, is to hear the word and to hear others talk about their testimonies. It is so important to be around positive people, especially when you are going through a hard place. Negative people will sap your faith right out of you, but positive people will build upon the faith level operating in your life. Who are you hanging around with?

When a battle crosses my path, I do not call someone who is going to die in battle with me but someone who is going to help lead me through to victory. Who are you calling? We are supposed to be calling up, not calling down! You have no business calling anyone just to tell them your sad story. You need to have a network of people who will stand with you and cover you when you don't feel like praying. You need a network of people who are positive and not negative and who see the end instead of what is happening right at that moment. If you do not have people in your life like this, start praying for God to show you who these people are and ask Him to lead them to you and you to them. Believe me, He will honor that request. Just do not be distracted and miss them once they are before you.

We may need some help being tucked into rest. Rest in Him! Sometimes, we will need someone to sing us a sweet lullaby of God's hope, grace, and mercy, in order for us to have that peace that surpasses all of our natural understanding and gives us the ability to rest in him.

Meditation Thought

I challenge you to:

Rest in Him when you know that you have done all that He has asked for you to do pertaining to your situation.

I challenge you to:

Examine who you are around.

I challenge you to:

Examine who you are calling.

I challenge you to:

Examine who you are listening to.

I challenge you to:

Make the necessary adjustments in order for you to rest in Him.

My Thoughts

OPEN TO ADJUSTMENTS

As I was praying, God began to speak to me about goals and purpose. He showed me that sometimes we become so purpose (goal) oriented that we are not open to adjustments. We need to learn to make these adjustments as situations and circumstances present themselves.

Personally, as I have walked in my purpose, I have been faced with distractions as well as redirections (adjustments). We have to realize that sometimes what we think is a distraction is a redirection and vice versa. I know you are saying, "Oh boy! That's nice to know, but how do I distinguish the difference?" Well, the first thing I do is breathe. Yes—breathe! Take a deep breath and look at where this situation came from and how it fits or doesn't fit into my divine purpose.

If you take time to think about it, it is easy to tell the difference between a distraction and a redirection. A distraction will take you away from your purpose, and a redirection will enhance the direction you are already traveling in.

I recently had a distraction cross my path. Its whole purpose was to distract me away from my purpose. I knew what it was because it brought confusion and turmoil with it. I recognized it and continued to move forward in my purpose.

I also recently have had a redirection cross my path. I knew what it was because it brought with it another avenue in pursuing my purpose. I still had to make the choice if I wanted to trust God with the redirection or stay right where I was. I chose to trust God. This redirection required me to become even more diligent with my time management.

We have to be open to redirections. They are designed to add another facet in our unique design. The "redirection road" can lead you further along in your purpose than you ever imagined.

I want to encourage you to be open to adjustments because, through the adjustments, God's perfect alignment for purpose will manifest for your life.

Meditation Thought

I challenge you to:

Take a deep breath when faced with a circumstance or situation that may be either a distraction or a redirection.

I challenge you to:

Allow God to bring the needed adjustments into your purpose.

I challenge you to:

Not become legalistic in your purpose, but rather open to the adjustments that God places before you.

My Thoughts

LIVING: LAW OR GRACE?

God showed me that many people are confessing that they live by grace, yet they are residing under the law. You feel you have all sorts of rules and regulations that you have to maintain in order for God to love you and bless you. This is bondage!

Jesus died on the cross for every sin we could ever fall into. He took our punishment so we could live with grace. Jesus was able to bear this because He knew His father loved Him. Jesus set a new covenant into place, a covenant of grace. Grace is not a thing; grace is a person—Jesus.

God tells us His number one command is love. Mark 12:30–31 (NKJV):

> *And thou shalt love the Lord thy God with all thy heart, and with all thy soul, and with all thy mind, and with all thy strength: this is the first commandment. And the second is like, namely this, Thou shalt love thy neighbor as thyself. There is no other commandment greater than these.*

We are to first love God. He gave us this commandment, and Christ is in us. We have to receive God's love within ourselves.

You have to receive God's love, for this is the only way you will live knowing God loves you. If you do not have the revelation that God loves you, no matter what you do or don't do, you do not love yourself. If you have asked Jesus into your heart to live, you are born again. Your spirit man has been awakened. In that awakening, you are covered in the blood shed by Christ on the cross. God sees only this good in you; He does not see your shortcomings and your failures. He sees the grace and love that he so freely gave you.

Have you truly experienced the love of God? Do you understand that it is not about performance and the list of do's and don'ts? We, as lights representing God in this world, have to first understand love. For God so loved the world . . . the greatest of these is love. If we could love ourselves, we would not have issues with judging others because we would see that if not for the grace of God, if not for Jesus, that could be me!

We need to stop finger-pointing, debating the word, and alienating people who don't believe the way we do. We need to stop spewing hatred at homosexuals, calling women who walk into abortion clinics "baby killers," and grow up in God's love. Imagine this—you receive a revelation of God's love, and instead of shoving scriptures down someone's throat, you love them. You live the word in front of them, and one day, because you showed them grace instead of the law, they come to you and say, "No one has ever treated me like you do. You listen to me and you do not judge me. You tell me straight, yet all I feel is the love behind what you are saying to me."

This is possible, but first, you have to receive the gift of grace into your life. God loves you, and you cannot do anything to change that. I mean anything! When we have the revelation of grace in our lives, it is going to cause us to want to set down the sin in our life, not continue in it. If you are operating under the law, you are operating under condemnation, and you will continue to sin because you are telling yourself, "God could never love and bless me. I am a mess-up."

Again, God's love is not dependent on your performance. God's love is there—always unconditionally—just waiting for you to receive it. Will you receive it today?

Meditation Thought

I challenge you to receive God's love. How? Meditate on the grace that He has so freely given you.

Meditate on the truth that your performance has nothing to do with whether or not God is or is not going to love you.

Selah—pause and think of that!

My Thoughts

_____
_____
_____
_____
_____
_____
_____
_____
_____
_____
_____
_____
_____
_____
_____
_____
_____
_____
_____
_____
_____

GOD'S PROTECTION

Last Monday morning, as I was stepping into the shower, I slipped on the marble and down I went. I knocked my head on the corner of the bathtub. I began to cry out for my husband. I had not realized that I had cut the back of my head until he came in and told me to move my hand. He began to pray for me and helped me up with an ice pack on my head. I am the type of person who sees stars and feels sick at the sight of my own blood. My husband helped me to sit down, and once the nausea passed, I got up and went back to the shower, got in, washed my hair—cut and all—and proceeded to get ready for the day. I did not have a headache, and besides needing to keep pressure on it until the bleeding stopped, I was fine.

I shared this story in order to show my point, that God's protection is greater than we can comprehend. My injury could have been a lot worse. I could have broken a bone, hurt my back, or even knocked myself out. God protected me when I was not expecting the unexpected. How many times has God protected you when the unexpected took place?

I know that when I pray, the blood of Jesus washes over me and I am protected. I also know that there are many individuals who pray for me because God lays me on their hearts. I am protected. I know I have angels encamped around me, protecting me. I know that I am hidden under the shadow of His wing. When the unexpected happens, I know that His protection is . . .

God loves you so much that He is constantly protecting you. You are His cherished, His beloved!

Bask in His love and protection. He does not protect you because of what you do. He protects you because He loves you!

Meditation Thought

I challenge you to:

Reflect on all the times God has protected you; not just physically, but in all areas of your life.

I challenge you to:

Be thankful—just be thankful in all things!

I challenge you to:

Bask in God's love and protection for you!

DEBRA CAMPANY

My Thoughts

_____
_____
_____
_____
_____
_____
_____
_____
_____
_____
_____
_____
_____
_____
_____
_____
_____
_____
_____
_____

BY GOD: LOVE IT IS

God is love. If I could pour one thing into you, it would be God loves you no matter what. When I say no matter what, it means *no matter what!*

Because of some of our upbringings, understanding and receiving God's agape love has been difficult. I come out of abuse, and to comprehend that someone could love me without a performance was almost too much for me to get my natural mind around. I always felt like I needed to be doing or perfecting something in order for God to love me and bless me. I finally, after many years, have an understanding that God loves me no matter what.

We hear that phrase—God loves me no matter what—and do not know what to do with it. Some of you right now are growing uncomfortable with the thought of God loving you just because you are you. As humans, we have a wrong perception of what God's love is. When we are in relationships, we have a tendency to put strings on our love. If you don't hurt me, I will love you. If you do this for me, I will love you. If you love me, I will love you. This is not God's love. This is a polluted love that has been formed due to our upbringing, our perceptions, our definition of love.

We need a "love overhaul," and the only way that is going to take place is by receiving the agape, unconditional love that only comes from God. Once we receive that, we will love ourselves because we will take all of our self-imposed expectations and trade them in for His grace, His righteousness, His mercy, and His love.

Without the agape love of God, when you fall, you will be accused and condemned. This is a sure sign that you have not received the agape love of God. When you receive the love of God and you fall, you will get right back up because you understand that you are cloaked with God's righteousness, not self-righteousness. Jesus paid the price for all of our sins. He took the punishment. He was judged for all sin so we don't have to be. We are under grace, and when we understand this and receive this, we will come to realize that everything He says we can have according to His word. It is already ours; we just didn't have the rhema revelation of it.

My prayer is that you have a rhema revelation of just how much God loves you, just because you are you.

Meditation Thought

I challenge you to:

Meditate and think about how much God loves you. He does, no matter what!

My Thoughts

DISTRACTION OR REDIRECTION

God has been speaking to me concerning purpose and how sometimes circumstances or situations that cross our paths are not distractions, but rather redirections. That is powerful, I thought. We have been taught that everything negative that comes across our path is a distraction. A lot of times that is true. Yet there are times when something happens that is actually God using that situation to cause a redirection in our purpose. This causes us to snap out of that comfort zone of one-way thinking.

I want to share a personal experience with you. I pray that this will help you recognize if you encounter a distraction or redirection. Something happened in my life that could have caused me to sit down and not move. I had to take a moment and be still long enough for God to reveal to me that this was a distraction and that I was to continue moving forward in the direction that He had set before me. I did just that. I was not taken out of the race due to the distraction. Instead, it caused a redirection to take place.

"What do you mean, Reverend Debra?"

I mean that if I had sat down and given up because of the distraction, I would have to go around that mountain one more time. Because I didn't succumb to the distraction, but rather, continued to walk in my purpose, it has caused a redirection to take place. I now understand how my purpose can be fulfilled, even when circumstances and situations in my life say contrary.

We get it in our heads that when God says something to us we have to be dogmatic about it. In other words, there is no room for us to move outside of the box that we have put God in. God took what was meant for my destruction (the distraction) and turned it into good for me. I am now preparing to enter into a new arena, and God is showing me how I can continue to move forward in ministry and still be able to fulfill another assignment I have in my life. I can look at it now and chuckle at myself, thinking I knew things were going to be a certain way. I realize now it was never going to be certain because when God is leading my footsteps, just as He leads yours, He may tell me to sit one day and leap the next. That is why it is all about obedience. The only thing we can be certain of (pertaining to purpose) is that all things work for our good when we walk according to His purpose.

It is important to make sure your spiritual life is first in your life. We will be faced with many distractions to try to steal us away from our purpose, but we also have to be open to the redirections that God sends to us when He wants us to proceed to His best for us. If Joseph had not listened to God in Matthew 2:12 when Herod was trying to kill Jesus and had returned to Herod instead of moving in a different direction (a redirection), Jesus would not have been able to fulfill His purpose. Joseph could have thought he heard a distraction and said, "No, we are returning to Herod," but he took it as a redirection. Once Joseph was redirected (he had departed to head back to his own country), God appeared to him in a dream and told him to flee to Egypt and stay there until He brought word. Herod was seeking the young child to destroy Him. Joseph obeyed the redirection again and stayed in Egypt until Herod was dead. We are fruit of Joseph's obedience to the redirection in his life.

I am humbled by the revelation that God has shared with me concerning purpose and distractions and/or redirections. He showed me just how human we are and how much we need Him in our lives to discern every turn, every mountain, every valley, and every pasture.

Meditation Thought

I challenge you that the next time you are faced with what appears to be a distraction, to take a moment to examine it and listen to God's direction before reacting to it. Then be obedient to what He is telling you to do.

My Thoughts

_____
_____
_____
_____
_____
_____
_____
_____
_____
_____
_____
_____
_____
_____
_____
_____
_____
_____
_____
_____
_____

POWER IN A PAUSE

What is the power in a pause? One of the definitions of pause (www. dictionary.com) is: *a temporary stop or rest.* Sometimes, it is good to pause in your process. It is good to take a temporary stop or rest.

Have you ever had to drive a long distance? If you are on a major highway, you will notice that there are rest stops along the way. We are on a long journey and are traveling a long distance in this life. That is why sometimes you need to pause temporarily in your process in order to be refreshed, to reflect, to be still and know that He is God.

Some of us are known as "doers." We do not consciously take the time to smell the roses. Others of us may get stuck in the pause instead of using it for what it is: temporary. I would challenge you this week to determine which personality you are and focus on pausing if you are a doer and doing if you are a pauser who is stuck in temporary stop.

I would consider myself a "doer," so I have to make a conscious decision to take pauses in my journey. Otherwise, I would be like the Energizer Bunny who just keeps going and going and going and doing and doing and doing. I would deplete all my God power and run out of gas, only to be broken down on the sideline of my journey.

When we pause in God, there is peace, time, direction, or redirection. There is placement, purpose, protection in the pause, and there is power in a pause.

Meditation Thought

I challenge you to:

Examine yourself to discover if you are a "doer" who takes no time for yourself. If so, do one thing for yourself this week. You have to take care of yourself or you will not be any good to others.

Come on, you are worth it!

I challenge you to:

Examine yourself to discover if you are a "pauser" and you cannot seem to get going and you feel as though you are in a rut. If so, do one thing this week that you know will be a step out of the pause.

Come on, you can do it!

My Thoughts

_____
_____
_____
_____
_____
_____
_____
_____
_____
_____
_____
_____
_____
_____
_____
_____
_____
_____
_____

RECOGNIZING YOUR PAIN

God showed me that one of the keys to recognizing your pain is the ability to see beneath the symptoms, the surface.

I experienced this lesson firsthand. Not long ago, a little pain surfaced in my life that I had thought was healed. I discovered my symptoms were manifesting and I had not recognized them. What God began to show me was that sometimes He allows us to walk in the emotional healing that has been revealed to us only to reveal more healing when we are able to handle and process it.

I have never agreed with revisiting old wounds just to reopen them, I agree with the Holy Spirit, who asks us to allow the pain to be recognized as He reveals it to us. I believe that true healing comes when God does the work. God may use individuals in your life to help you with this process, but you are the only one who can deal and heal from the past pains. No one else can do that for you.

God is the one who began the work in you, and He will be the one who completes it. There are seasons in healing. You may go through a season where you recognize your pain and deal with it, and thus you are able to heal. Then you enter a season of rest where you walk in the healing that has been exposed to you. The problem we have is that we try to force our process. We don't know how to be gentle on ourselves in our process. Do not allow fear to keep you from recognizing your pain.

Know that this is your season of recognition. We are growing from glory to glory and from level to level, and as we do, God will help us to recognize our pain in order to gain His abundant life!

Meditation Thought

Meditate on recognizing your pain and what that statement means to you!

My Thoughts

THE BLESSING IN THE MIDST

I immediately thought about all the times I didn't want to do what was asked of me, but when I did, there was always a blessing in the midst of it.

Years ago, I was injured in a car accident. I had to go through all sorts of tests and was on all different types of prescriptions. I always gave praise, and I loved to dance before the Lord. However, the pain that I had suffered was a hindrance to me in my praise to Him. During a service, God spoke to my pastor and asked him to tell me to dance and my healing would manifest. I did not want to dance; I hurt. I chose to be obedient, and I danced with all I had in me. I felt awesome and I felt free. When I got home, I felt immediate and horrible pain. My head and back were screaming. My husband held me and prayed silently. All I could say was, "I am healed, I am healed," as I fell asleep. When I woke up, the pain was gone for good! I went to church that evening as a testimony to God's blessing in the midst.

If I had not been obedient and done what was asked of me, I would have missed that opportunity for my healing to manifest. By faith, I set aside what I thought and felt and obeyed what was asked of me. In the midst of being uncomfortable, God made my healing manifest.

Is what has been asked of you to do outside your comfort zone, your area of comfort, out of your box? Could it be that in the midst, God wanted to manifest that blessing? You cannot go back. I challenge you that the next time you are asked to do something for Him or by Him, do it and see what manifests in the midst of it.

Meditation Thought

Set aside your feelings of being uncomfortable and do what God is asking you to do.

Get a rubber band. Keep it before you as a reminder of how stretchable and resilient you are.

Look for the blessing in the midst.

My Thoughts

_____
_____
_____
_____
_____
_____
_____
_____
_____
_____
_____
_____
_____
_____
_____
_____
_____
_____
_____

GOD CAN—NOT CAN GOD?

Jeremiah 32:37 (KJV) reads:

> *Behold, I am the Lord, the God of all flesh: is there any thing too hard for me?*

Do you think you may be limiting God? According to the Oxford Dictionary, the definition of *limited* is confine within definite limits, restricted in scope, extent or amount, set bounds to.

Are you saying, "Can God?" instead of "God Can"?

The Lord spoke to me concerning the season we are in and how we often say, "Can God?" Our minds and spirits may be saying God can, but our actions and words are saying "Can God?" When we speak loud with our actions, we are doubting that He can

Believe me! I understand how easy it is to get distracted by the pressures of daily life and to actually begin to let doubt creep in. This is why I truly believe God is asking you to get back to foundational teaching of your youth. What does this mean? It means getting back and remembering what we were taught when we were first saved.

Remember when everything was possible and you grasped hold of every word you heard and you actually put it into practice? We have to make a conscious decision to hear what God is saying in this season. Could it be He is saying that He can? He can be and do above and beyond all that we could ask or think, but we are limiting what He can do because of our own thinking and perception of our lives.

We have all been there. We have said or done certain things that hinder our progress in our purpose. But let's change our confession. Let's change our actions. Let's change our perceptions. Let's say, "God Can." We have to stop looking at our situation as a dwelling place—it is only temporary—and when we dwell there, we are asking "Can God?" instead of declaring "God Can."

One thing I have found out in this race that I am running is that things never work out the way I think they are going to. Things always work out for my good because my God can.

Can you believe Mark 9:23 (Amp):

> *And Jesus said, You say to Me, If You can do any-thing? Why, all things can be (are possible) to him who believes!*

I dare you to!

Meditation Thought

I challenge you to:
Change your actions and confession from Can God? to God Can!

I challenge you to:
Read and meditate on Mark 9:23.

I challenge you to:
Not limit God—He is limitless.
Selah—pause and think on that.

My Thoughts

_____

_____

_____

_____

_____

_____

_____

_____

_____

_____

_____

_____

_____

_____

_____

_____

_____

_____

WAITING ON MANIFESTATION I

God is up to some interesting things, and waiting on manifestation is one of the most interesting for us. God gives us numerous scriptures to stand on. Here are just a few:

James 1:4 (KJV) reads:

> *But let patience have her perfect work, that ye may be perfect and entire, wanting nothing.*

Galatians 6:9 (KJV) reads:

> *And let us not be weary in well doing: for in due season we shall reap, if we faint not.*

Romans 8:28 (KJV) reads:

> *And we know that all things work together for good to them that love God, to them who are called according to his purpose.*

You may be saying, "Great, Reverend Debra! I needed that reminder. But this is tough and it is difficult not to look at my circumstances. I feel as though I am up to my neck in lack, and I am trying to keep my head above water."

This is going to hurt your flesh, so if you can't look past your flesh, stop reading this now! Otherwise, please proceed. In a prophetic word from God spoken to me on 3/18/2009 at 9:20 A.M., God told me this:

"It is time, Beloved, to set aside what you see and to operate in what I say. No longer can you get by on a bottle filled with milk and a pat on your back to make you feel better. I am calling you to a higher level of glory. But only those who are willing and obedient will progress to that new level. Patience and perseverance is a necessity in this season, so is a higher level of thinking. Put on my mind," sayeth God. "Put on my strength," sayeth God. "For those of you who cannot see beneath the surface will get lost at sea. Stop listening to and believing everything you hear and read just because of who is saying it. I am speaking to you, but you cannot hear what I am saying because you cannot see beneath the surface of the stormy seas. You are giving your ear to other sources."

Peace is yours in this season if you choose it. Your soul can prosper in this season if you choose it.

Choose this day whom you will serve: God (your first love), or your situation (your distraction, your pity point)?

Serve God! Deal with your situation and wait for God's manifestation—His promise—and be patient in the process, for He is at work.

Selah. Pause and meditate on the word of the Lord.

Meditation Thought

I challenge you to reread this week's reflection every day this week.

My Thoughts

_____
_____
_____
_____
_____
_____
_____
_____
_____
_____
_____
_____
_____
_____
_____
_____
_____
_____
_____

WAITING ON MANIFESTATION II

God is not allowing me to get off "waiting on manifestation." I believe it is because there are a lot of you wondering and longing for different things to manifest in your lives, and He wants to use this meditation as a tool for you to understand the manifestation process.

You play a major part in the manifestation process—it's called obedience.

Many of you do not realize that you hold your destiny in your own hands. It is your decision whether to do what God is asking of you. Faith without works is dead. You cannot sit on the couch and expect the tomatoes in the field to be harvested. You have to do whatever you believe God is asking you to do. When you know you have done all that He has told you, you stand and rest in knowing He is at work on your behalf.

If He asks you to arise, go forth, and act on something, then do it! If He says turn right, do it! If He says stop, then do it! Don't make your walk complicated. His word says that it is simple enough for a child to understand. Maybe we need to study children in order to recognize some things within ourselves, amen! When a child is trained properly and taught how to do things and disciplined in certain areas, they know they should obey their parents. When they are told no, they stop. When they are told go, they go. They are obedient to the voice of their parents.

We need to be obedient to the voice of our Father. It is really quite simple, isn't it? If only our own will would stay out of the way! Selah—pause and think on that!

Meditation Thought

I challenge you to:
Get out of your own way.

My Thoughts

WAITING ON
MANIFESTATION III

I believe God wants you to receive a revelation of the manifestation that is about to take place in your life! We have to run this race with faith, perseverance, patience, perseverance, purpose, perseverance, obedience, perseverance, joy, perseverance, thanksgiving, and perseverance. I believe you understand what the Holy Spirit is saying.

You cannot run a race if you do not have the stamina to endure the course. The definition of *stamina* (www.dictionary.com) is: *the power to endure*. The definition of *endure* (www.dictionary.com) is *to bear with patience, to hold out against, to continue to exist*.

Wow! We can look at it this way—God gives us the power to endure with patience the course that is set before us—the course to the manifestation of the promise, of our purpose, of our destination, of the finish line. Every trial, every tribulation, is designed to become a testimony. A testimony of not only God's goodness but of the increased stamina and endurance that comes with everything we go through. Know that your stamina is increasing in this time of testing. With stamina increase comes patience to endure the physical effects of the manifestation process that will result in the spiritual promise.

My desire is to run my race that is set before me and to see the manifestations of my destiny unfold as I press, push, and pursue with patient endurance everything that crosses my path.

What is your desire? Do you want a quick fix or do you want a lasting manifestation? One that will last for generations to come. Jesus had a lasting manifestation when He paid the price on the cross.

Because of His sacrifice, we are still manifesting salvation today. It has not run out and it never will!

Be patient and wait on the manifestation. In due time, you will reap the benefits, if you do not faint, give up, or settle for the quick fix.

Focus on the promise (the prize), not the problem. Deal with the problem!

Meditation Thought

I challenge you to:

Build up your cardio workout. It will increase your stamina and endurance.

Not so many individuals like to work out, but it is healthy for us and it is for our good. The trials and tribulations you go through are to build up your "spiritual cardio." Once you get through this, you will know that you can do all things through Christ who strengthens you!

When faced with a challenging situation or circumstance, I challenge you to repeat the following at least ten times per day (or when a negative thought comes into your mind). Watch your focus change and your strength increase:

You can do all things through Christ's strength.

My Thoughts

WAITING ON
MANIFESTATION IV

Let's be real! When we are pressed on every side and faced with one negative report after another, we can grow weary and get tired and worn out to the point of just throwing our hands up in the air and saying, "Enough, I give up." Well, let's look at that statement. Enough, I give up—let's turn it around on the enemy and use it for your good, amen!

God's Word reads in 1 Peter 5:7 (KJV):

Cast all of your cares upon Him, because He cares for you!

Maybe we need to get to the point where we do throw our hands up in the air and say, "Enough, I give up," in order for God to be able to move freely in our lives and manifest all that He has for us.

"Reverend Debra, you have discussed doing all things through Christ which strengthens me, now you are telling me to throw my hands up in the air. Did it occur to you that you need God's strength in order to throw your hands up in the air and give it up to Him?"

Some of us don't know when to stop. We would keep on keeping on and end up worn out, tired, and not able to think clearly. We beat ourselves up because we think we should be able to handle things, when God is waiting for us to turn it over so He is able to manifest His desire for our life.

It should be so easy when we hear, "Cast all of your care upon Him, because He cares for you." Yet due to fear of letting go, we don't make this decision. We think as long as we are in control, everything will be OK. No! We have to learn that in order for God to manifest what He has promised us, He has to be in control.

You will know when it is time to throw your hands up in the air and say, "Enough, I give up!" No person can tell you when it is time for you to surrender that which you have been in control of to God. That is between you and your Daddy.

Know that He knows all that you are facing, feeling, and dealing with, and it is your Daddy's desire to carry you through your manifestation, so allow Him to do this for you.

Meditation Thought

I challenge you to:

Examine your heart and mind, and if you are in the place of saying, "Enough, I give up," then go ahead and give up. Give it up to God, and watch the manifestations as you release the care you have been carrying.

My Thoughts

_____

_____

_____

_____

_____

_____

_____

_____

_____

_____

_____

_____

_____

_____

_____

_____

_____

_____

_____

_____

WAITING ON
MANIFESTATION V

I want to discuss the timing process of manifestation and how everyone's timing is different, just like your fingerprints.

I once heard a comparison between our purpose becoming manifested and the train system at Atlanta's airport. The doors to the train and the terminal open at the same time, and once we step into the train, we are transported into another terminal very quickly. The timing of the doors has to be in sync. If the doors on the train don't open but the ones in the terminal do, you still cannot get on the train and vice versa. If God opens the door for your manifestation and you are not in position, you will miss the opportunity—all due to timing.

We seem to have issues with our timing gears. We want it now, but God is saying not yet, you still have some growing to do. Or he may be saying now is the time and we drag our feet because of fear. Some people would rather walk from terminal to terminal at Atlanta's airport than step between those synchronized doors onto the train! They will still get to the destination, but it will take them a longer time.

Ecclesiastes 3:1–8 (NIV) reads:

> *There is a time for everything, and a season for every activity under heaven: A time to be born and a time to die, a time to plant and a time to uproot, a time to kill and a time to heal, a time to tear down and a time to build, a time to weep and a time to laugh, a*

*time to mourn and a time to dance, a time to scatter
stones and a time to gather them, a time to embrace
and a time to refrain, a time to search and a time to
give up, a time to keep and a time to throw away, a
time to tear and a time to mend, a time to be silent
and a time to speak, a time to love and a time to
hate, a time for war and a time for peace.*

God has a time for everything, and timing in the manifestation process is just that—a process. You were predestined before the
foundations of the world. That means God already has every one of
your mistakes factored into your destiny. So stop focusing on where
you think you have missed it and realize you have not missed a thing,
because God already knew your doors were not going to open when
His did. Instead, focus on your next footstep and on obedience to
His leading. Have peace in knowing your manifestation will happen,
and your doors and His doors will open at the same time!

God's purpose will be manifested in your life.

Meditation Thought

I challenge you to:

Go easier on yourself in your manifestation process. Remember we operate in grace. So receive God's grace and watch how you will see the manifestation of His promise to you, His purpose for you, and His timing fulfilled in you!

My Thoughts

_____
_____
_____
_____
_____
_____
_____
_____
_____
_____
_____
_____
_____
_____
_____
_____
_____

ARE YOU TURNING FROM
OR TURNING TO?

Are you turning *from* or turning *to*? If we are constantly focused on what we are turning from—our past, our sin, or even our successes— they can be a hindrance to our future. If we are focused on what we are turning to, we are focusing on our possibility, our God consciousness. Turning from and turning to are both the same action. It is just our perception that determines what we are focused on.

Notice I said "focus." The definition of *focus* (www.dictionary.com) is: *a central point, as of attraction, attention, or activity, to concentrate.* I like "as of attraction," because where you are focused is the direction you will travel. You will attract what you are focused on. Are you turning *from* or turning *to*?

It is so easy to be focused on what we need to turn from that we become engulfed by the negativity that surrounds that thing that is taking up our thoughts. We can also be so caught up in what God did for us and long to be back there that it becomes a hindrance to where He wants to take us. I am not saying don't remember what God did, I am saying don't be focused on it, because that is where you will stay, back there in what He did.

God's Word reads in Philippians 4:8 (AMP):

> *For the rest, brethren, whatever is true, whatever is worthy of reverence and is honorable and seemly, whatever is just, whatever is pure, whatever is lovely and lovable, whatever is kind and winsome*

and gracious, if there is any virtue and excellence,
if there is anything worthy of praise, think on and
wait and take account of these things.

Think on good things. Think on what you are turning to instead of turning from. Be focused on what is ahead of you and not behind you. You cannot move forward if you are constantly focused on what is behind you.

Are you turning to a new attitude? Are you turning to a new course? Are you turning to a new goal? Are you turning to a new direction in your life? Focus on these things and not what you turned from. An example would be turning from cursing. If you are so focused on the cursing, it will continue to be big in your life. But if you turn to speaking what is pure and learning a new way of dealing with the frustration that causes the cursing, the new way will become big in your life.

Another example is someone who used to own his own business and now is working as an employee for someone else. Instead of focusing on what he lost in his business and his freedom to work for himself, he should focus on what God would have him learn as he works under new authority.

It is all your own perception of whether you are turning *from* or turning *to*.

I have to make a daily choice that I am turning to Jesus and His way or else I would constantly be focusing on what I was turning from, and that would beat me down and keep me out of all He has for me.

Choose today whom you will serve. What/who are you turning from or what/who you are turning to?

Meditation Thought

I challenge you to:

Stand up and face to the left (representing the past).

Now turn to the right (representing your now and future).

Do you feel it? You are making the decision at this moment that you will focus on what you are turning to and you are choosing to leave the past behind. Do this exercise as often as you need to as a reminder, an action of faith, to change your mind-set to turning *to*.

My Thoughts

_____

_____

_____

_____

_____

_____

_____

_____

_____

_____

_____

_____

_____

_____

_____

_____

_____

A THING CALLED WILL

I had a conversation recently with someone on the topic of will. Who is will? What does will have to do with anything? How does will work?

God will not force you into his will for your life. It is all about your freedom of choice. Have you ever heard the phrase "a strong-willed child?" That was me. I knew what I wanted and no one could move me off it. Being this way has been both a blessing and a curse. When you are strong-willed, I believe you have a built-in discipline and self-control system. This is a problem if I am following *my* will instead of God's, and I end up taking the long way around every time.

Who is will? The definition of *will* (www.dictionary.com) is: *the faculty of conscious and especially of deliberate action; the power of control that the mind has over its own actions: Freedom of the will.*

Will is your freedom of choice.

What does will have to do with anything? It has everything to do with everything. Will is diligent, purposeful determination. It is self-control and self-discipline. Your will determines your direction. Are you surrendered to God's will for your life (which makes His will your will), or are you running the show?

How does will work? It works by choice. You hold the key in your hand. It is the choices you make today that affect your tomorrows. Jesus, while in a place called Gethsemane, Matthew 26:39 (NASB) *fell on his face and prayed, saying, My Father, if it is possible, let this cup pass from me, yet not as I will, but as you will.*

John 6:38 (NASB) reads:

> *For I have come down from heaven, not to do my*
> *own will, but the will of Him who sent me.*

Every decision you make and every direction you walk determines your destination. Even Jesus had to make a decision concerning a thing called will. I have a choice and you have a choice. God is not going to force you to choose His plan for your life. That decision is totally up to you. God may set you up, but it is still your decision to follow His will for your life.

Which one *will* you follow?

Meditation Thought

Surrender your will to His will. I know, easier said than done. But practice, practice, practice, and watch what happens!

My Thoughts

BULL'S-EYE FAITH

One of the ways to release your faith is when you focus your mind on a specific target. Let's call it the bull's-eye.

In 1 Kings 17:9–12 (KJV):

> *Then the word of the Lord came to him (Elijah)*
> *to arise and go to Zarephath and dwell there. God*
> *had commanded a widow there to provide for him.*
> *Elijah focused his faith on getting to Zarephath, and*
> *the widow was at the entrance of the city gathering*
> *sticks. Elijah called to her asking for a cup so he*
> *could drink, and as she was going to get it he called*
> *to her to bring him a morsel of bread. She replied*
> *that she did not have bread, only a handful of flour*
> *in a bin and a little oil in a jar. She told him she*
> *was gathering the sticks to go in and prepare it for*
> *herself and her son so they could eat it and die.*

The widow was in a dying position—a faithless, fearful position due to her circumstances. Elijah told her not to fear, but to go and do as she planned, but also make him a small cake from it first and bring it to him. Then, afterward, make some for herself and her son. For as Elijah told her, "The Lord says, 'The bin or flour shall not be used up, nor shall the jar of oil run dry, until the day the Lord sends rain on the earth.'" She went away and did what Elijah told her to do, and they all ate for many days. The bin of flour was not used up

128

and the jar of oil did not run dry, according to the word of the Lord spoken by Elijah.

The widow focused on the word of the Lord (the bull's-eye), and it released faith to create that which she was focused on.

Her life was not all peaches and cream. After she moved forward in faith, there were still issues in her life. Her son became sick and he died (1 Kings 17:17–24). She was upset in verse 18 (KJV) it reads:

The woman said to Elijah, Why did you ever show up here in the first place—a holy man barging in, exposing my sins, and killing my son?

Have you ever felt like that? Even Elijah cried out to God and said why have you brought tragedy on the widow who made a place for me, killing her son? For a moment, they were both in a dying position, but then Elijah did what he felt he needed to do and the Lord heard him.

The child lived and the widow woman knew Elijah was a man of God and that the words in Elijah's mouth were truth. You would think that she would have known this when he supplied the flour and oil, wouldn't you?

Does anyone else other than me sometimes forget what God has already done and what He has already provided for us? I am being real.

Sometimes, when it comes to the good things God has done for us, we have a mental blackout due to the circumstance, issue, or care at hand.

Sometimes, we may be off target as we shoot for the bull's-eye, but we can refocus and remain focused on the bull's-eye of our faith and watch as it manifests.

Meditation Thought

Remain focused on the bull's-eye!

My Thoughts

ENOUGH IS ENOUGH

Have you ever gotten to the point of saying, "Enough is enough?"

I have. I believe that sometimes we actually have to get to that point in our lives because it is at that point that we will begin to make the necessary changes that will challenge us to continue to move forward in God's purpose and destiny for us.

How many times have you allowed someone else to affect your destiny? Notice I said "have you allowed." How many times have you complained to someone about what you are tolerating in your life? Notice I said "complained," not sharing your heart, asking for help, and so on. There is a difference. If you are complaining about it, then you are not operating in grace. You either have to change the way you are looking at the situation or get out of it. If you hear from God concerning your situation and He is telling you to endure, then He has already given you the grace to be in it and endure it. If you are in a situation and you are enduring by your own strength, instead of listening to God, it quite possibly could take you out.

Sometimes in situations where we get to the point of saying enough is enough, we realize we can no longer cosign someone else's issues. It is at this moment, we can make healthy decisions for ourselves and continue to move forward.

Please understand that even when we hear from God, we still can have "enough is enough" moments. Once we have rested, we again see God's plan and purpose and continue to press on through to the other side of the situation.

I've often heard the phrase, "When you get sick and tired of being sick and tired, you will do something about it." That is an "enough is enough" moment. Only you can make the decision to either suck it up and continue to press forward or stop complaining about something you are tolerating and move forward in God's purpose and plan for your life!

Only you know the answer to your "enough is enough" moment. No one can tell you what to do or not to do, not even God. But He can and He will lead you, and only you know which way He is leading you.

Meditation Thought

Examine your "enough is enough" moment and ask yourself the following questions:

1. Am I in this situation because of God's leading or because of my own (grace vs. flesh)?

2. Am I complaining about this situation because I am tolerating it or because I am just experiencing a weak moment and need to rest and regroup?

3. Do I have a word from God concerning my situation? If not, seek Him for one.

My Thoughts

_____
_____
_____
_____
_____
_____
_____
_____
_____
_____
_____
_____
_____
_____
_____
_____
_____
_____

PRESS ON THROUGH
TO THE OTHER SIDE

Have you ever wanted to stop pressing? Have you ever been so tired, worn out, or emotionally exhausted that you wanted to stop pressing and give up? I have. I know firsthand how easy it would be just to lie down and not get up. We are called to press on through to the other side. We are called to forget that which is behind, which could be anything that could be a hindrance to you moving forward.

Philippians 3:12–14 (NIV) reads:

> *Not that I have already obtained all this, or have already been made perfect, but I press onto take hold of that for which Christ Jesus took hold of me. Brothers, I do not consider myself yet to have taken hold of it, But one thing I do: Forgetting what is behind and straining toward what is ahead, I press on toward the goal to win the prize for which God has called me heavenward in Christ Jesus.*

I know that sometimes in the "pressing" we can grow weary; that is why it is so important to have a support system. I have said this before and I will say it again—we need one another. When I am tired, you can lift my arms up. When you are tired, I can do the same.

The problem we run into is that we don't trust one another due to past experiences, hurts, and betrayals. We have to trust God with one another, and in that, we have to know that the motive in our hearts is what God looks upon. If we are pure in our hearts concerning what we confide in someone, we have to know that God has us covered, even if the person severs our trust. I am speaking from experience. I have had my trust tossed aside, stepped on, and literally crushed, yet if I did not continue to put myself out there, being transparent, I would have missed some of the most special relationships. We as humans have the tendency to base relationships on past experiences. Yet God's word tells us to forget the past. If we continually base a new experience on a past experience, it actually *is* the past experience because you are just reliving the past.

We have to press on through to the other side of our pain, our hurts, our disappointments, our failures, our victories, our issues. The decision is yours—what will you decide?

Meditation Thought

Press on through to the other side by asking for help putting yourself out there again, because this time could be the time. Trust God with your heart

He will not let you down!

My Thoughts

_____
_____
_____
_____
_____
_____
_____
_____
_____
_____
_____
_____
_____
_____
_____
_____
_____
_____

BEHIND THE SCENES

The verse 1 Samuel 16:7 (NKJV) reads:

> *But the Lord said to Samuel, Do not look at his appearance or at his physical stature, because I have refused him. For the Lord does not see as man sees; for man looks at the outward appearance, but the Lord looks at the heart.*

I am glad God does not look at our outward appearance, our outward actions, or our outward reactions. I am thankful He looks at our heart. Imagine if we could grab hold of this principle. Imagine if instead of us looking at the situation or circumstance in our lives, we looked beneath the surface at what is happening behind the scenes. We tend to look at the outer appearance instead of the under (inner). I wonder what someone would see if we could open our hearts and let them read them. What would we see if we stopped looking at the outer and started seeing beneath the surface of the hurts, expectations, lack, motives, etc.? What would we see?

I am thankful that God sees the potential and gifting he placed within me. I am thankful he looks within me and does not judge me according to the shortcomings of my flesh, but rather according to my heart. I am thankful that He never gives up on me, but rather encourages me to pull myself up by the bootstraps and run the race set before me. I am thankful that He is constantly working behind the scenes.

We serve an under-the-surface God. Whatever He is doing is happening in the spirit long before it manifests in the physical, and sometimes, that can be a long process. I want to give you an example. Have you ever looked at your circumstance and tried to help God manifest what you wanted to occur, only to find yourself in a bigger mess? I have, and I came to the realization that I was totally operating in my own strength. God knew I was going to try to help Him out, yet He was still operating behind the scenes. He was working all things out for my good.

Oh, beloved, if we would allow ourselves to see behind the scenes and beneath the surface, I truly believe that we would see as God sees and love as God loves. Each of us is on a journey called life, and we all have our own processes to walk through. It could be a peaceful process in the midst of the storm if we could grasp that God is working behind the scenes on our behalf and that it will work out for our good. It is the good that God sees as good for our life.

The decision to look behind the scenes is yours. What will you decide?

Meditation Thought

Look beneath the surface of your circumstance, your situation, and see what God is doing in you. Grasp hold of this truth that God is working behind the scenes on your behalf and the end result is good!

My Thoughts

GOD'S DO POINT

When I walk out to my vehicle in the mornings, I walk through the dew. God started to speak to me concerning His *do* point. I love how God uses something as simple as dew to proclaim a word of encouragement.

When I looked up the definition of *dew point* in dictionary. com, I found it very interesting. It stated that in order for the dew to be formed, pressure was needed. In other words, the pressure you are experiencing in your life is going to cause your do to manifest.

Just like we all have a breaking point, we also have a do point. We all come to a place where we make the decision to do what God has asked of us. It is at the "do point" that change occurs. Sometimes, all we have to do is make the decision to act and the manifestation begins. Have you ever had that happen? You make a decision, and before you even make a physical movement in that direction, the manifestation occurs.

You may be at the breaking point in your situation. Your breaking point is actually your do point, and you will arise, go forth, and take hold of all that God has asked of you.

Your "do" is your faith in action. We are not only to be hearers but doers. It is time to move into all God has designed for your life.

Are you at your "do point" yet?

Meditation Thought

I challenge you to:

Break if you need to break—once you have your "do," the process can begin and change will occur.

I challenge you to:

Examine where you are in your life and determine if you are at your "do point." If you are, put the action plan into motion and walk into your destiny.

I challenge you to:

Not just be a hearer and just talk about what you are going to do, but be a doer and change your talk into your walk!

My Thoughts

DE-STRESS

God revealed to me that when we are in distress, we need to know how to de-stress.

Stress in our life causes us to become distressed. The definition of *distress* (www.dictionary.com) is: *great pain, anxiety, or sorrow; acute physical or mental suffering; affliction; trouble.* It sounds like stress to me. One of the definitions of *stress* (www.dictionary.com) is: *physical, mental, or emotional strain or tension: Synonyms: anxiety, burden, pressure, worry.* It is amazing how similar these definitions are.

We have stress in our life. The verse 1 Peter 5:7 (KJV) reads, to *cast all of your cares upon Him, because He cares for you.* It sounds easy, doesn't it? Let's be real. When we are hit from every direction and feel as though the weight of the world is upon us, we may stand there saying, "How do I do this, Lord? How do I give this to you?"

His answer may be, "One step at a time, one thing at a time, because I love you and I will never leave you nor forsake you."

We need to learn how to de-stress. The definition of *de-stress* (www.dictionary.com) is: *to reduce the emphasis.* That means when things in our life cause us stress, we need to not focus on the stress. We need to focus on the solution. There are times when we must deal with situations and circumstances of life, but do not allow yourself to be consumed by them. You need to implement a de-stress plan and know what you are going to do when the distressing things happen. When you de-stress, you are able to see and hear clearer. Your picture of your situation may change. Implement your plan, whether you go to the beach, play a sport, go for a walk, or even to take a bubble bath. The key is to do whatever works for you to de-stress. You need to do it!

Meditation Thought

I challenge you to:

Not get caught up in the drama of daily life (including other's dramatic situations). These affect your ability to see and hear clearly!

I challenge you to:

Implement a de-stress plan.

My Thoughts

_____
_____
_____
_____
_____
_____
_____
_____
_____
_____
_____
_____
_____
_____
_____
_____
_____
_____

SCARS

As you travel through life, you will experience many kinds of wounds. These wounds may leave scars, but the scars are only there to serve as a reminder that you are human.

When Jesus arose from the dead, He had scars from where He had been nailed to the cross. These scars were a symbol of what He went through in order to bring us freedom. His scars were a symbol of how human we are. In fact, Jesus's scars proved to doubting Thomas that He really was Jesus. Thomas said:

> *Unless I put my finger into the imprint of the nails and my hand into his side, I will not believe* (John 20:25, NKJV).

Thomas touched the nail pierced hand and put his hand into Jesus's side. Do you think Jesus's wounds were open and bleeding? No, there was scar tissue there. Jesus paid the price for our sin. Isn't it amazing how God allowed Jesus's scars remain so Thomas would believe? God could have removed the scars, but Jesus's scars were used to show what He had been through.

What about you? Have you been trying to remove your scars? Have you been trying to be the perfect believer? I am here to set you free! God allowed you to go through your wounds just like He allowed Jesus too. This is so you can be a hope to someone else you meet and help set the captives free. Whatever you have been through in your life, it has been for someone else. I do not know about you, but I want to shorten someone's journey, and if they can learn from my experiences and it helps them to better themselves, then everything that I have been through and every scar I have received is worth it.

Do not despise your scars. They are someone else's hope. Your scars are someone else's freedom.

Meditation Thought

I challenge you to:
Stop hiding your scars under bandages!

My Thoughts

_____
_____
_____
_____
_____
_____
_____
_____
_____
_____
_____
_____
_____
_____
_____
_____
_____
_____
_____
_____

I WILL NOT REFUSE

"I am only one; but still I am one. I cannot do every-thing, but I still can do something. I will not refuse to do the something I can do" (Helen Keller).

What can you do today to make a difference in someone else's life? Can you offer a word of encouragement or buy them a cup of coffee? The one little something that you can do will make a difference in someone else's life and, in turn, in your own.

I have come to the conclusion that I will not refuse to do what I can do. Like Helen Keller said, "I may not be able to do everything, but I can do something."

What is your excuse? You don't like the person? Do they rub you the wrong way? You don't like their tactics? Yet God is telling you to do something for them. What is your excuse? I know this is challenging, but the real challenge is listening to what God is asking you to do and setting aside your emotions. It can be difficult to set aside what you see and remain obedient to what God is asking of you.

I want to use myself as an example. I have been helping my husband start a new business. I go to work with him at least three days a week. Am I getting a paycheck for this? No. I am doing what God asked me to do—something. As I do, I am "sowing" my time into my husband's dream. I am doing something to help him. I cannot do everything, but I can do something. I know that as I am obedient to do the "something" God told me to do, someone will do something for me and my dream.

I will not refuse! What about you?

Meditation Thought

I challenge you to:

Do something, because even though you are one, you can make a difference!

There was a man walking along a beach where thousands of starfish had washed ashore. As he walked, he would reach down every few steps and pick up a starfish and throw it back into the ocean.

A young man walked by him and said, "What are you doing? You can't possibly make a difference."

The man replied as he picked up a starfish and threw it into the ocean, "I made a difference to that one!"

My Thoughts

NO MATTER WHAT

What do you do when the going gets tough? Sometimes, all we have left is our determination to say, "No matter what, Lord, I will serve you."

Have you ever had someone walk out on you when you were in the midst of what you considered one of the lowest points in your valley? I have. What do we do when this happens? Sometimes, it is as simple as just saying these three very powerful words—*no matter what.*

Most of the time, it is on us to pick ourselves up and continue to press on. We have a tendency to rely upon one another, sometimes in unhealthy ways. I cannot look to my husband to fulfill what God has planted in my heart as my purpose. He can help me, but I cannot put the manifestation of my destiny upon him. The same goes for any of my friends or family. I have to have the unction within myself to allow God to mold me, squish me, and sometimes slam me down and start the reshaping process all over again. That is when my "no matter what" comes into play.

When everything is going according to our plan, life is grand. But when everything is going contrary to our plan, life is a letdown. Whose plan are you following? Did it ever occur to you that God has to get you to a place of total surrender to His will? That is the place of "no matter what."

Jesus experienced this in the garden as it says in Luke 22:42– 44(KJV):

He said, "Father, if thou be willing, remove this cup from me: nevertheless not my will, but thine be done." And there appeared an angel unto him from heaven, strengthening him. And being in agony he prayed more earnestly: and his sweat was as if it were great drops of blood falling down to the ground.

Our "no matter whats" are broken. We faint before we can be strengthened. We faint because we try to endure the agony in our own strength, or we look to others who fail us in their own human state. Jesus went through this process and finally looked to God to strengthen Him. Sometimes, God is the only one who can encourage you, cheer you on, lift you up, and set your feet upon solid ground. He will never leave you nor forsake you.

I have come to the conclusion that I have to proclaim just as Jesus did: "No matter what!" I will fulfill the Father's will for my life. What about you?

Meditation Thought

I challenge you to:

Examine yourself this day.

Be honest about what you are experiencing emotionally, and if you discover that you are looking in the wrong place for your strength, then refocus on the One who gave you breath and press on through no matter what.

My Thoughts

_____

_____

_____

_____

_____

_____

_____

_____

_____

_____

_____

_____

_____

_____

_____

_____

_____

_____

_____

AN AHA MOMENT

Have you ever experienced an "aha" moment? That moment when a lightbulb goes off inside you? That moment when you receive the download straight from the Father? I have, and it is in that moment when clarity, understanding, and wisdom all occur at once.

An aha moment is a life-altering moment. It is a moment in time when you know beyond a shadow of a doubt that what you just experienced is going to change or confirm the direction you are traveling in. I believe there are those of you that have experienced these moments but could not put a name on them. Well, now you can, and now you can expect more aha moments to manifest in your life. I also know that some of you know exactly what I am referring to—a Rhema word from God.

Whether you call it an aha moment or a Rhema word, it is a moment in time that comes alive to you and changes your life. I do not know about you, but with all of the negativity that we can be faced with on a daily basis, we need to receive Rhema words from God. We need to receive those aha moments that encourage us, challenge us, and catapult us into our destiny. Walk out your moment. Live in your moment. Expect your moment to lead you to your next level of glory in God's plan for your life.

Recognize the moments God gives you and embrace them, because God created everything good and He is working all things out for your benefit.

Expect your aha moments.

Meditation Thought

I challenge you to:

Meditate on past moments that you may have passed by because you did not recognize that they were aha moments.

I challenge you to:

Once you recognize the moment, embrace it, be thankful for it, and watch what happens.

Man says, "We missed it," but God says, "You will get it next time!"

My Thoughts

_____

_____

_____

_____

_____

_____

_____

_____

_____

_____

_____

_____

_____

_____

_____

_____

_____

_____

YOU ARE BLESSED

In 3 John 2 (KJV) we read:

Beloved, I wish above all things that thou mayest prosper and be in health even as they soul prospers.

To me, this means that the most important thing to God is that my soul prospers. Once my soul prospers, all other areas of my life will follow suit. I am not only blessed, but those around me are blessed because of God working in me.

Do you realize that you are blessed? I feel that we have a twisted idea of what it means to be blessed. We look at it in the realm of the natural (things) instead of in the spiritual. In order for us to have the true prosperity that God is talking about, it has to begin inside of us. He wants us healthy physically, emotionally, spiritually, mentally, and financially—basically in all areas of our lives. Seek Him first and then all things will come. We want the things before the healing of our character, but that cannot be. It would destroy some of us. God always knows what is best for us.

You are blessed even in the midst of your circumstances. Your character is being shaped and molded into what God needs it to be.

You are blessed even in the midst of that outburst of flesh you just experienced. It has been designed to cause your soul to prosper.

You are blessed even in the midst of wishing you were someone else. It is His desire to bring forth your gifts that have been dormant within you and help you to recognize how valuable you are to Him and His purpose for you.

You are blessed even in the midst of your world appearing to fall apart. He has you in the palms of His hands, shaping you, forming you, and loving you.

You are blessed! It is up to you to determine this within your heart and decide to follow God's leading and direction. Watch what He does for you!

Meditation Thought

I challenge you to:

Proclaim that you are blessed no matter what and that you are willing to pay the price for your soul to prosper.

My Thoughts

_____

_____

_____

_____

_____

_____

_____

_____

_____

_____

_____

_____

_____

_____

_____

_____

_____

AGREE TO DISAGREE

What happens when you have a disagreement with someone and they try to manipulate your way of thinking to agree with theirs? Unless we can be mature enough to agree to disagree, we can become distanced and divided from that person. It would be wonderful if everyone I come into contact with on a daily basis would agree to disagree. But let's be real here. The possibility of this occurring is rare because of our perception of agreement.

God's word says that we are to be in one accord, in unity. I truly believe that He did not mean that was at the expense of my belief system. What if it is as simple as agreeing to disagree and moving forward from that point? It is about the attitude of your heart and if your motive is pure and just.

Think about this. Most of the time when we disagree with someone, we try to persuade them to our way of thinking. This can be frustrating as well as manipulative. You may have actually experienced this on the other end of the disagreement as well. What if, instead of trying to make someone agree with us, we simply stated, "Let's agree to disagree on this point." I believe in that moment of agreeing to disagree, there is a unity that happens. In that unity, we are accepting one another, and in doing so, we allow God to do his work.

I personally do not want "yes" people in my life. Where is the accountability in that? Where is the challenge if everyone in my life always agrees with everything I say and do? Is that healthy? I do not believe so. Some people are purposely placed into our lives to challenge us to a higher level and to add an accountability aspect to our lives that otherwise may not be present. Instead of embracing the "sandpaper people" in our lives, we want them out. They make us feel uncomfortable or bring things out of us that we would not otherwise realize was still present unless that challenge button had been pressed.

I firmly believe that in the ability to agree to disagree there lies freedom for God to work on individuals at His pace and not at our pace. I know that it is OK for me to disagree with individuals in my life and that it is OK for them to disagree with me. Disagreeing with someone does not mean you do not believe in them. So many times, offense is taken because the individual feels as though the person disagreeing with them is doing so because they don't believe in them or what they feel God is asking of them.

We need to stop buying into the lies of the enemy and keep him under our feet where he belongs! Agree to disagree and watch what God will do!

Meditation Thought

I challenge you to:

The next time you are faced with a disagreement, rather than argue, agree to disagree and see what God does in the situation.

I challenge you to:

Look within yourself and be honest. Do you embrace the "sandpaper people" God has placed in your life, or do you run every time you see one coming toward you? Be honest! Stop running because God is up to something!

My Thoughts

THE GAME CALLED LIFE

Do you remember that board game Life? This game originated in 1860 and has evolved over the years, just as your game called life evolves and progresses with each passing day. We are to go from glory to glory, from challenge to challenge, from revelation to revelation, from change to change, and from old ways to new ways (His).

We are to navigate the life we have been entrusted with as if we are a ship being navigated by our captain (God). When the captain is aware of a hazard, such as a storm up ahead, he steers the ship around it or he has a plan to navigate the ship through what lies ahead. That is comparable to us. As we navigate the game called life, we are to allow the Father to navigate us around the hazards, storms, and circumstances that may be ahead. We get into trouble when we attempt to navigate ourselves. When we get in the way, we may end up shipwrecked on the shore, wishing we had listened to our captain. The good news is that He already has those wrecks factored into our lives. He already knew that we would get stuck on the sandbar instead of going around it when He told us to. He already knew that we would hit that reef that cuts us wide open as His living water fills us and we sink into His graceful and loving arms.

In the game called life, your responsibility is to listen to the direction of the Father and be obedient to His voice. As your footsteps are ordered by Him and He directs your path, you will become all that He intended you to become. You will touch all the people that He intends you to touch in the game of life!

Meditation Thought

I challenge you to:
    Live your life!

My Thoughts

DISTRACTIONS CAN
BE DISASTROUS

The definition of *distraction* (www.dictionary.com) is: That which distracts, divides the attention, or prevents concentration: that which amuses, entertains, or diverts; amusement; entertainment: division or disorder caused by dissension; tumult.

Proverbs 4:25–27 (AMP) reads:

> *Let your eyes look right on [with fixed purpose], and let your gaze be straight before you. Consider well, the path of your feet, and let all your ways be established and ordered aright. Turn not aside to the right hand or to the left; remove your foot from evil.*

Do not look to the left or to the right, but keep your eyes focused on what is ahead of you! Do you realize that distractions can be disastrous if you do not recognize them for exactly what they are? They are designed to take you off course away from your Godly gifts, your Godly talents, your Godly purpose, and your Godly anointing.

Have you ever noticed that if you are driving a car and you get distracted by something on your left side, it isn't long and the car is moving to the left? That is what happens in our lives when we start looking at that "thing" rather than focusing on God and His plan for us.

Distractions come in all shapes and forms. You may be distracted by people in your life who want you to become a part of their

175

drama. Be watchful! You may be distracted by wanting to have fun, fun, fun all the time. Be watchful! You may be distracted by something that appears to be a good thing when actually it is taking you away from God's purpose for your life. Be watchful! I believe you get what I am saying. What distracts me may be a blessing to you. Each of us is different from the other and our lives are very different.

You will recognize when a distraction appears in your life. I know when a distraction has appeared in my life because it brings a sense of being out of my element, or even at times, confusion comes. I get the sense that I should not be giving this all my time and energy. We are not to think that every unplanned thing that happens to us is a distraction. It is our responsibility to seek God concerning the situations, circumstances, and people that arise in our lives. We have to trust that He will show us, lead us, and guide us when we are willing and obedient to listen.

Be watchful and guard yourself against distractions, because if left unrecognized, distractions can be disastrous to God's plan and purpose for our lives.

Meditation Thought

Take a few moments of quiet time to ask God if there are any distractions in your life that need to be dealt with and then deal with them!

My Thoughts

I DARE YOU

As a kid, I used to play "truth or dare" with my friends. I would get to choose if I wanted truth or dare. It is funny to think back on it now. I chose truth most of the time because I was not a very daring individual. I had this one friend who always chose dare because she loved to be dared to do stuff. It was a very interesting game, to say the least. Are you a risk-taker? This is an area in my own life that God has done tremendous work in. As I said, I always chose truth over dare because I was a chicken when it came to taking a chance, but not anymore. The great One resides on the inside of me, and greater is He that is in me than he that is in the world!

Are you a risk-taker? Do you need to develop this area as I had to? Either way, you can do it! Sometimes when you are naturally a risk-taker, you can be somewhat reckless. When you are naturally reserved, you can be somewhat afraid to make any movement. Let's talk about balance and listening to what God is asking of you.

Matthew 14:26–31 (KJV) reads:

> *And when the disciples saw him walking on the sea, they were troubled, saying, It is a spirit; and they cried out for fear. But straightaway Jesus spake unto them, saying, be of good cheer; it is I; be not afraid. And Peter answered him and said, Lord if it be thou, bid me come unto thee on the water. And he said, come. And when Peter was come down out of the ship, he walked on the water, to get to Jesus. But when he saw the wind boisterous, he was afraid;*

and beginning to sink, he cried, saying, 'Lord, save me,' and immediately Jesus stretched forth his hand, and caught him, and said unto him, O thou of little faith, wherefore didst thou doubt?

When Peter walked on the water, he was a risk-taker. I can imagine that he thought, *I would rather be a wet water-walker than an afraid-to-get-out-of-the-boat timid person.* There is one thing in particular in this passage of scripture that I want to focus on that I believe is going to get the "I dare you" across to you and set you free. In verses 28 and 29, Peter put the Lord to the test. He said, "If it be thou, bid me come unto thee on the water."

Hey, Jesus, if it is really you, dare me to come and I will walk on the water just like you.

Jesus answered, "Come, and when Peter was come down out of the ship (comfort zone), he walked on the water, to go to Jesus." If Jesus is daring you to come, then go, start, do it. Even if you end up realizing, *I am walking on water and the waves and wind are big,* He is going to be right there to scoop you up!

I dare you to do all that God asks you to do. I dare you to not let your situation or circumstances keep you out of that which you know God has asked of you. I dare you not to look at your finances or your needs when He tells you to give. I dare you to love when it seems impossible, and to laugh when you have nothing to laugh about. I dare you to love the gift that God has instilled on the inside of you. I dare you to enjoy your journey because this is not your final destination.

I dare you…

Meditation Thought

I dare you to:

Trust God and lean not to your own understanding of what is happening in your life!

My Thoughts

ARE YOU IN THE FOG?

I was in a revival meeting once, and the preacher shared with us about the FOG—"favor of God," and I got thinking about how we really should be walking around with our heads in the clouds. Are you in the FOG? Are you in the favor of God? If you are in Christ, the favor of God is available to you. You just need to do your part. You should not only receive all God wants to offer you, but be obedient to what He is asking of you. When He speaks to you, He is trying to get something to you so it can move through you.

I want people to notice that my head is in the clouds. The clouds represent the FOG, and I want to receive all God has for me. Favor is not fair and it is not just. In our own strength, we can do nothing to receive the favor of God. His favor is just that—favor.

Do you realize how many times God's favor has operated in your life? Favor is better than material things. Favor is a connection that God gives you that opens up a whole new world to you. Favor is speaking to that bill collector on the other end of the phone and having a time extension granted or a bill forgiven. Don't always think that favor is going to be money-related. Yes, it can be, but we limit God's ability to pour out His favor upon us because we are not looking in all of the places He has placed His favor for us to find.

We get lazy in the treasure hunt and only look at the surface. Come on, people, let's start lifting up those rocks, looking in those fish's mouths, moving those mountains, and walking with our heads in the FOG. Come on, you can do it. Are you fed up yet? Are you tired of the same old routine yet? Come on, you can do it! God hasn't called you to lie on the couch and wait for that job to appear. Go recreate yourself through the FOG. Keep knocking, keep walking, keep pressing until the door opens, and do not take no for an answer. As you pursue God, you will catch Him and all He has for you. Today is what you make it. Make it a day that counts for the pursuit of your purpose.

Meditation Thought

I challenge you to:

Think on the FOG—favor of God—and look for it in places that you wouldn't normally look.

I challenge you to:

Move outside of the world you have created and enter into the world God has created for you!

My Thoughts

PSALM 91

Psalm 91 (Amplified) reads:

He who dwells in the secret place of the Most High shall remain stable and fixed under the shadow of the Almighty [Whose power no foe can withstand].I will say of the Lord, He is my Refuge and my Fortress, my God; on Him I lean and rely, and in Him I trust! For [then] he will deliver you from the snare of the fowler and from the deadly pestilence. [Then] He will cover you with His pinions, and under His wings shall you trust and find refuge; His trust and His faithfulness are a shield and a buckler. You shall not be afraid of the terror of the night, not of the arrow (the evil plots and slanders of the wicked) that flies by day, Nor of the pestilence that stalks in the darkness, nor of the destruction and sudden death that surprise and lay waste at noonday. A thousand may fall at your side, and ten thousand at your right hand, but it shall not come near you. Only a spectator shall you be [yourself inaccessible in the secret place of the Most High] as you witness the reward of the wicked. Because you have made the Lord your refuge, and the Most High your dwelling place. There shall no evil befall you, nor any plague or calamity come near your tent. For He will give His angels [special] charge over you to accompany and defend and preserve you in all your ways [of obedience and service]. They shall bear you up on their hands, lest you dash your foot against a stone. You shall tread upon the lion and adder; the young lion and the serpent shall you trample under- foot. Because he has set his love upon Me, therefore will I deliver him; I will set him on high, because he knows and understand My name [has a personal knowledge of My mercy, love and kindness—trusts and relies on Me, knowing I will never forsake him, no, never]. He shall call upon Me, and I will answer him; I will be with him in trouble, I will deliver him and honor him. With long life will I satisfy him and show him My salvation.

God laid it on my heart to share this chapter with you and to tell you I personally recite this daily. I often put in the names of my loved ones, friends, or anyone in need of God's deliverance. Are you willing to make a difference not only in your life but in the lives of those around you?

This day, I want to suggest to you to do the same. Commit to it for a period of at least thirty days and watch the freedom that comes into your life!

Meditation Thought

I challenge you to:

Read Psalm 91 for at least thirty days. In place of each *he*, *I*, *you*, and so on, put in the names of those you are lifting up in prayer, including yourself, and look what the Lord will do.

DEBRA CAMPANY

My Thoughts

LOOSE THAT...
AND LET IT GO

John 11:44 (KJV) reads:

> *And he that was dead came forth, bound hand and foot with grave clothes: and his face was bound about with a napkin. Jesus saith unto them, "Loose him, and let him go."*

What or who do you need to loose in your life and let go? Recently, I had to loose some situations and circumstances and release them into God's hands.

If you are overwhelmed with trying to help someone out, it is you instead of God doing the work. But any work that you do that is not of God will only fade away. God's work will last for generations. I would rather have God working on my behalf and rest in His word and trust that the battle is not mine but His.

Just like I had to, you need to loose that person and let them go. You need to loose that circumstance and let it go.

The definition of *loose* (www.dictionary.com) is: *free from anything that binds or restrains.* Imagine that. Do you understand that when you wrap someone up in your expectations, your demands, your idea of what you think they should do, you are actually wrapping them into grave clothes (bondage)? The definition of *let* (www.dictionary.com) is, *to allow or permit: to allow to pass, go, or come.* The definition of *go* (www.dictionary.com) is, *to become as specified, to move or proceed, to leave a place; depart.*

Let us examine this closer. Loose him and let him go! Free him and allow him to become all that God intends him to become. My goodness, could it be that because of your involvement with the people in your life that you are keeping them bound up? Could it be that because of your involvement with the circumstances that you are keeping the situation bound up? Loose them and let them go! Allow God to work in that person's life or in your situation, but you have to set them free for them to become all God intends.

Notice one more thing. Lazarus did not unwrap and loose himself; rather the people around him loosed him and unbound him from his grave clothes. I believe that it is up to us to make sure that the only hands we have on another person are the obedient hands of God that are unwrapping them. We need obedient hands that loose them and let them go. Those around Lazarus had obedient hands. They had hands that did as Jesus told them to do.

Set someone or something free today and watch the freedom you receive in return.

Meditation Thought

Whether it be a spouse, a child, a friend, a parent, grandparent, a sibling, a coworker, whomever, I challenge you to:

Loose that individual and let them go to become all God intends them to become. For God loves that person far more than you ever could.

I challenge you to:

Loose that situation and let it go so that God can work it all out for good on your behalf.

Be obedient.

DEBRA CAMPANY

My Thoughts

_____
_____
_____
_____
_____
_____
_____
_____
_____
_____
_____
_____
_____
_____
_____
_____
_____

PEACE IN THE STORM

You can have peace in the storm. It is possible to have peace when the waves are pounding and tossing your boat to and fro. It is possible to arrive at your destination as you discover through your journey to release it to God and to move into His wisdom, His knowledge, and His plan for you.

Could it be that the storm is designed for that purpose? Could it be that the storm is designed to move you into God's will and out of yours? Could it be that the storm (the storm that God already knew in advance was headed your way) was designed to bring you to another place of trusting Him? You can have peace in the storm, but the decision is yours.

Psalm 107:25–30 (Amp) reads:

> *For he commands and raises up the stormy wind, which lifts up the waves of the sea. (Those aboard) mount up to the heavens, they go down again to the deeps; their courage melts away because of their plight. They reel to and fro and stagger like a drunken man and are at their wits' end. Then they cry to the Lord in their trouble, and he brings them out of their distresses. He hushes the storm to a calm and to a gentle whisper, so that the waves of the sea are still. Then the men are glad because of the calm, and he brings them to their desired haven.*

I believe one of the key ingredients to having peace in the storm is realizing God is there with you.

"Reverend Debra, how can God be with me when I am messing up?"

His word says that He will never leave you nor forsake you. What does that mean? He leaves you if you fall back into sin? He leaves you if your flesh is weak and you cannot stand like you thought you should? No! Absolutely—no! He says He will never leave you nor forsake you. He is married to the backslider. That means that He must have known that we would all have issues. Marriage is a covenant. Imagine that. You bought the lie that you are alone. You are not alone. God is with you. Jesus is right there, just waiting for you to get to the place where you have the revelation that you can have peace in the storm! A storm in your life does not necessarily mean you are doing something wrong. A storm may come because you are heading in God's direction and into His purpose. The enemy of your soul doesn't want you arriving at your destination. Yes, you can have peace in the storm, and finding that peace is a journey only you can walk. It is right there in front of you. Reach out and grab it and receive it, in Jesus's name.

Meditation Thought

I challenge you to: Be still and know that God is God.

Be still long enough to allow God to show you His peace in the midst of the storm.

Be still and be quiet. Because in the quietness, in the whisper, you will see His peace.

My Thoughts

WHAT HAVE I TO GIVE?

Have you ever been in the place where you ask yourself, *What have I to give?* Could it be that you are there right now? Maybe you feel totally poured out, drained, nothing left to give, and you don't know what to do. I have been there a number of times. I would like to say you only visit this place once, but that would not be true.

I know that when I have given my all and have nothing left to pour out; it is in that moment when I am my weakest that I feel God's strength rising up inside of me. You probably thought that I was going to talk about having nothing to give financially. That is a whole different message. I want to talk about you and when you have done everything you know to do and still it appears nothing has changed. I want to talk about you and when you have stood your ground and you do not feel as though you could go through another day. Yet you continue to stand.

What have I to give? Today, the answer may be nothing. Tomorrow is a new day. What have I to give? Can I muster a smile for someone else's sake? Can I find a kind word? You cry out to God, "I do not know. What have I to give?" Could it be that you are emptied out so that you have room to receive what God has to give you? Could it be that today is your day to receive? Why do we look at situations and circumstances that enter our lives as a negative? Could it be that you are at your lowest so He can raise you to His highest?

Isaiah 40:31(AMP) reads:

> *But those who wait for the Lord shall change and renew their strength and power; they shall lift their*

wings and mount up as eagles; they shall run and not be weary, they shall walk and not faint or become tired.

What have you to give? How about a word that sounds on the inside of you saying that you will make it. A word that God is right there with you in your emptiness and brokenness drawing you close. A word that changes you and renews your strength so that you will soar to heights you have never encountered before.

Receive all He has for you in this hour.

Meditation Thought

I challenge you to:

Rest in Him knowing what you have to give. How about time to allow Him to work things out in your life, time to draw Him closer to you so He can lift you up!

My Thoughts

MARY AND MARTHA:
WHO ARE YOU?

Are you a Mary or a Martha? Are you a doer like Martha? Are you like Mary, about to take a moment to sit at the feet of Jesus and listen to what He has to say?

Luke 10:38–42 (KJV) reads:

> *Now it came to pass, as they went, that he entered into a certain village: and a certain woman named Martha received him into her house. And she had a sister called Mary, which also sat at Jesus' feet, and heard his word. But Martha was cumbered about much serving, and came to him, and said, "Lord, doest thou not care that my sister hath left me to serve alone? Bid her therefore that she help me." And Jesus answered and said unto her, "Martha, Martha, thou art careful and troubled about many things: But one thing is needful: And Mary hath chosen that good part, which shall not be taken away from her."*

You could be thinking right now, *Reverend Debra, but I am doing for Jesus, what is wrong with that?* It is not that Jesus rebuked Martha for serving. He rebuked her for over-care in service. Meaning she was more concerned about the "doing" than she was about just sitting a moment and listening. Martha loved Jesus, received Jesus, served Jesus, believed in Him, had faith in Him, and she carried Christ's message to Mary. Martha was just caught up in the doing, doing, doing. The doing became a distraction and was robbing her of her blessing—hearing Jesus share the word!

Are you too busy doing what you feel is required of you to sit at Jesus's feet and listen to what He has to say to you? I know I have been there and I have done that. It is still challenging for me to balance this area in my life because I am a go-getter and a doer.

One thing I have learned is when I am working in my own strength, I fizzle out rather quickly. When I am listening and then doing, the anointing is there to accomplish all that He asks me to.

I am going to ask you again. Mary or Martha: who are you? Only you can truthfully answer that question!

Meditation Thought

I challenge you to:

Examine your heart and answer the question: Mary or Martha—who am I?

DEBRA CAMPANY

My Thoughts

HATS OF MANY COLORS

We wear hats of many colors. We have something on the inside of us that gives us the ability to change the color of our hats at any given time. Sometimes, we are businessmen or businesswomen. Sometimes, we are sons or daughters or husbands or wives. We are fathers or mothers, brother or sisters, or friends. Men and women may be running a business eight hours of the day only to switch into husband, wife, father, or mother mode when they get home. This makes us special. Do you understand just how special you are?

I was meditating on how I personally have had to change the color of my hat from one of businesswoman to one of wife and mother. This, of course, all has to be done within a matter of seconds, and most of the time, it is done without a conscious thought. When my kids were growing up, they didn't care if I was running an office by day, they needed Mom to fix them something to eat, make sure their homework was done, and that they were bathed and ready for bed. Then there was my husband who needed to have his special attention. There we go into the wife hat. Have you ever wondered how you are able to wear all of these different-colored hats? I have, and I have come to the conclusion that it is all by the grace of God.

God gives you the grace you need each day in order to accomplish that which is before you. He has gifted you with the ability to transform yourself in the twinkling of an eye. You can put on the color of hat that works for you in that moment.

Even though you wear hats of many colors, it is your responsibility to make sure that one of those hats has *your* name on it. Use the grace God has given you to take care of the main hat—you! If you are not caring for yourself, all the other colored hats you have to maintain will eventually pile on top of you and you no longer will be recognized for who you are but rather for all the hats that you wear.

Meditation Thought

I challenge you to:

Take a moment and reflect on your day and recognize the different colored hats you wear. Write them down if you have to. Then be honest with yourself and recognize if one of those hats has your name on it. If it doesn't, then make a conscious decision to add a new color to your wardrobe of hats—you!

Take time to minister to yourself!

DEBRA CAMPANY

My Thoughts

HOW TO KNOW GOD
PERSONALLY

Prayer is just talking with God. He knows your heart; don't worry about getting your words just right. Here is a suggested prayer to guide you:

Lord Jesus, I want to know you. I want to thank you for dying on the cross just for me. I give you my life, and I receive you as my Lord and Savior. Thank you for forgiving me of my sins and giving me the gift of eternal life. I ask you to take control of my life from this point forward. Make me the kind of person that you want me to be. I thank you for your love that is transforming me from moment to moment. In Your name I pray. Amen.

Did you pray just now to receive Christ as your Savior?

If so, congratulations! Do not forget this date.

ABOUT THE AUTHOR

By the grace of God, Debra's testimony includes her triumph over many years of sexual abuse and codependency. It is her heart to share with you her journey to freedom. Debra has shared her testimony in many different churches and through television. She crosses denominational lines, breaking down racial and religious barriers. She believes that the power of God's love builds a bridge over the gap in individual's lives.

Debra has used her past experiences to position her to now be able to bring encouragement, edification, teaching, giving, and the truth of God's Word and His Kingdom to others. Her heart is to empower individuals to prosper and become all God has ordained for them to become. She will challenge you, provoke you, correct you, encourage you, unlock your destiny within you, and love you through it.

Debra is an ordained minister and prophetess and knows firsthand the power of God's love.

Come join Debra on this journey, but only if you have the courage to prosper.

CPSIA information can be obtained
at www.ICGtesting.com
Printed in the USA
BVOW08s1250220318
511301BV00002B/335/P